CORE SKILLS

GRADE 2

Math

ISBN 0-7398-5724-X

2002 Edition, Steck-Vaughn Company
Copyright © by Harcourt, Inc.

Printed in the United States of America.

4 5 6 7 8 9 054 06 05 04

STECK-VAUGHN
ELEMENTARY · SECONDARY · ADULT · LIBRARY
A Harcourt Company

www.svschoolsupply.com

Core Skills: Math
Grade 2
Table of Contents

Core Skills: Math, Grade 2, Table of Contents (cont.)

Core Skills: Math, Grade 2, Table of Contents (cont.)

Joining Groups

Use the pictures.
Write the sums.

1. 4 + 5 = 9

2. 7 + 1 = ____

3. 3 + 6 = ____

4. 2 + 6 = ____

5. 5 + 2 = ____

6. 3 + 5 = ____

7. 4 + 2 = ____

8. 1 + 5 = ____

Number Sense

9. Which pair has the greatest sum?
   Ring the pair.

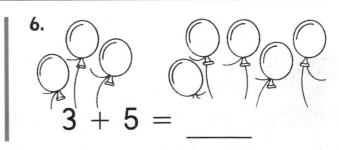

9 + 3   9 + 2   9 + 5   9 + 1

Order and Zero Properties

Write the sums.

1.
   $\begin{array}{r} 0 \\ +8 \\ \hline \end{array}$
   $\begin{array}{r} 8 \\ +0 \\ \hline \end{array}$
   $\begin{array}{r} 4 \\ +6 \\ \hline \end{array}$
   $\begin{array}{r} 6 \\ +4 \\ \hline \end{array}$
   $\begin{array}{r} 9 \\ +1 \\ \hline \end{array}$
   $\begin{array}{r} 1 \\ +9 \\ \hline \end{array}$

2.
   $\begin{array}{r} 5 \\ +3 \\ \hline \end{array}$
   $\begin{array}{r} 3 \\ +7 \\ \hline \end{array}$
   $\begin{array}{r} 7 \\ +6 \\ \hline \end{array}$
   $\begin{array}{r} 0 \\ +5 \\ \hline \end{array}$
   $\begin{array}{r} 2 \\ +6 \\ \hline \end{array}$
   $\begin{array}{r} 8 \\ +2 \\ \hline \end{array}$

3.
   $\begin{array}{r} 6 \\ +0 \\ \hline \end{array}$
   $\begin{array}{r} 9 \\ +3 \\ \hline \end{array}$
   $\begin{array}{r} 3 \\ +6 \\ \hline \end{array}$
   $\begin{array}{r} 0 \\ +4 \\ \hline \end{array}$
   $\begin{array}{r} 5 \\ +4 \\ \hline \end{array}$
   $\begin{array}{r} 9 \\ +0 \\ \hline \end{array}$

Visual Thinking

Ring the train that has the fewest cubes.

4.

5.

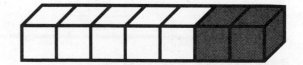

2

Adding on a Number Line

Draw lines to match.

1.

$1 + 6 = 7$

2.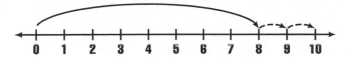

$3 + 6 = 9$

3.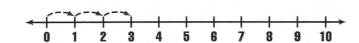

$0 + 3 = 3$

4.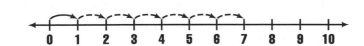

$5 + 4 = 9$

5.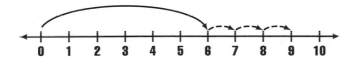

$8 + 2 = 10$

6.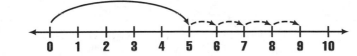

$6 + 3 = 9$

Story Corner

7. Tell a story.
   Write an addition sentence.

_____ + _____ = _____

_____ children

3

Counting On

Count on to add.

1. 8   6   5   8   7   9
   +2   +1   +2   +3   +1   +2
   10

2. 9   5   6   4   7   8
   +1   +3   +2   +2   +3   +1

3. 3   3   2   9   8   4
   +1   +2   +1   +3   +2   +1

4. 3   5   4   3   7   6
   +2   +1   +3   +3   +2   +3

Reasoning

Write the missing number.

5.
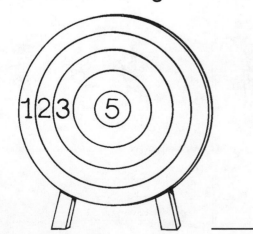

6.

4

More Counting On

Ring the greater number.
Then count on to add.

1.　　2　　　　8　　　　5　　　　1　　　　7　　　　3
　　+⑤　　　+1　　　+3　　　+6　　　+2　　　+7
　　 7

2.　　1　　　　3　　　　4　　　　9　　　　2　　　　2
　　+4　　　+4　　　+2　　　+1　　　+6　　　+8

3.　　2　　　　7　　　　8　　　　6　　　　3　　　　2
　　+9　　　+1　　　+3　　　+3　　　+5　　　+4

4.　　9　　　　7　　　　3　　　　2　　　　1　　　　3
　　+3　　　+3　　　+6　　　+8　　　+5　　　+1

Reasoning

Write the missing number.

5.

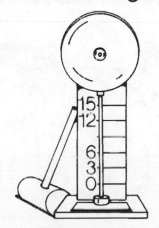

＿＿＿

6.

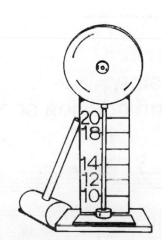

＿＿＿

5

Problem-Solving Strategy

Make a Model

Use the problem-solving steps to solve each problem. Use counters. Then write the number sentence.

Understand
Plan
Solve
Look Back

1. Sal saw 3 shows at the fair. Then he saw 2 more. How many shows did he see?

   $$3 \oplus 2 = 5$$

   _____ shows

2. Donna won 5 prizes. Then she won 2 more. How many prizes did she win?

   ____ ◯ ____ = ____

   _____ prizes

3. Donna had 6 tickets for rides. Hector had 3 tickets. How many tickets did they have?

   ____ ◯ ____ = ____

   _____ tickets

4. Hector saw 4 mirrors in the Fun House. Then he saw 3 more. How many did he see?

   ____ ◯ ____ = ____

   _____ mirrors

Story Corner

5. Tell a story.
   Write an addition sentence.

   ____ ◯ ____ = ____

   _____ children

6

Joining and Separating Groups

Use counters.
Write the number sentences.

1.

$$1 \,\oplus\, 4 = 5$$

2.

$$5 \,\ominus\, 4 = 1$$

3.

___ ◯ ___ = ___

4.

___ ◯ ___ = ___

5.

___ ◯ ___ = ___

6.

___ ◯ ___ = ___

7.

___ ◯ ___ = ___

8.

___ ◯ ___ = ___

Number Sense

9. Which number sentence has the greatest answer? Ring it.

$$10 - 2 = ? \qquad 10 - 4 = ? \qquad 10 + 2 = ? \qquad 10 + 4 = ?$$

Zeros in Subtraction

Subtract.

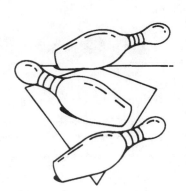

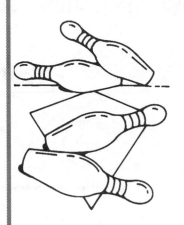

1. $3 - 3 =$ _0_	$5 - 0 =$ ___	$4 - 4 =$ ___
2. $6 - 0 =$ ___	$7 - 7 =$ ___	$9 - 9 =$ ___
3. $4 - 0 =$ ___	$6 - 6 =$ ___	$8 - 0 =$ ___
4. $8 - 8 =$ ___	$7 - 0 =$ ___	$1 - 0 =$ ___

5.

$$\begin{array}{ccccc} 2 & 3 & 1 & 9 & 5 \\ -2 & -0 & -1 & -0 & -5 \end{array}$$

Story Corner

6. Look at the picture.
   Make up a story problem.
   Ask a friend to solve it.

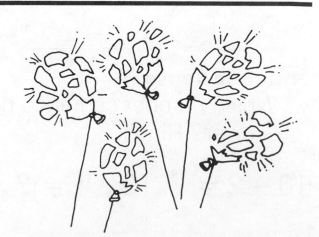

____ ◯ ____ = ____

8

Subtracting on a Number Line

Write the number sentence
that the number line shows.

1.

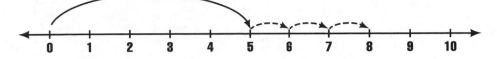

$$\underline{5} \enspace \left(\oplus\right) \enspace \underline{3} \enspace = \enspace \underline{8}$$

2.

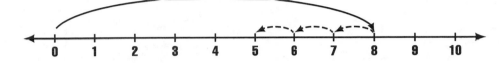

$$\underline{\hspace{1.5cm}} \enspace \bigcirc \enspace \underline{\hspace{1.5cm}} \enspace = \enspace \underline{\hspace{1.5cm}}$$

3.

$$\underline{\hspace{1.5cm}} \enspace \bigcirc \enspace \underline{\hspace{1.5cm}} \enspace = \enspace \underline{\hspace{1.5cm}}$$

4.

$$\underline{\hspace{1.5cm}} \enspace \bigcirc \enspace \underline{\hspace{1.5cm}} \enspace = \enspace \underline{\hspace{1.5cm}}$$

Visual Thinking

5. Ring the number line that shows subtraction.

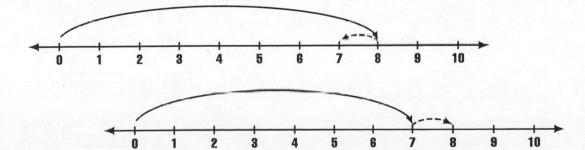

9

Counting Back

Subtract.

1.
$$\begin{array}{r} 6 \\ -2 \\ \hline 4 \end{array}$$
(6, 5, 4)
$$\begin{array}{r} 9 \\ -2 \\ \hline \end{array}$$
$$\begin{array}{r} 5 \\ -1 \\ \hline \end{array}$$
$$\begin{array}{r} 3 \\ -1 \\ \hline \end{array}$$
$$\begin{array}{r} 10 \\ -2 \\ \hline \end{array}$$

2.
$$\begin{array}{r} 7 \\ -1 \\ \hline \end{array}$$
$$\begin{array}{r} 4 \\ -2 \\ \hline \end{array}$$
$$\begin{array}{r} 8 \\ -2 \\ \hline \end{array}$$
$$\begin{array}{r} 2 \\ -1 \\ \hline \end{array}$$
$$\begin{array}{r} 10 \\ -1 \\ \hline \end{array}$$
$$\begin{array}{r} 5 \\ -2 \\ \hline \end{array}$$

3.
$$\begin{array}{r} 8 \\ -1 \\ \hline \end{array}$$
$$\begin{array}{r} 7 \\ -2 \\ \hline \end{array}$$
$$\begin{array}{r} 9 \\ -1 \\ \hline \end{array}$$
$$\begin{array}{r} 3 \\ -2 \\ \hline \end{array}$$
$$\begin{array}{r} 6 \\ -1 \\ \hline \end{array}$$
$$\begin{array}{r} 4 \\ -1 \\ \hline \end{array}$$

Problem Solving

Write a number sentence to solve.

4. Lou wins 4 bears.
   He gives 2 away.
   How many bears does
   he have left?

   ___ ◯ ___ = ___

   ___ bears

5. Sara sees 6 elves.
   Then 1 runs away.
   How many elves
   are left?

   ___ ◯ ___ = ___

   ___ elves

More Counting Back

Count back to subtract.

1. Say 10. (9, 8)

$10 - 2 = \underline{8}$

2. Say 8. 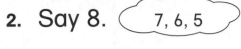 (7, 6, 5)

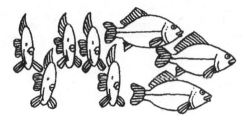

$8 - 3 = \underline{}$

3. Say 9. (8, 7, 6)

$9 - 3 = \underline{}$

4. Say 8. (7)

$8 - 1 = \underline{}$

5.
$$\begin{array}{cccccc} 9 & 9 & 10 & 8 & 9 & 10 \\ -2 & -1 & -3 & -2 & -3 & -1 \end{array}$$

Number Sense
Use a calculator.
Write the answer.

6. [**ON/C**] [6] − [2] − [2] − [2] = \underline{}

7. [**ON/C**] [8] − [2] − [2] − [2] − [2] = \underline{}

11

Counting Up

Ring the number that is less.
Then count up to find the difference.

1. $\begin{array}{r} 4 \\ -\,\textcircled{2} \\ \hline 2 \end{array}$ $\begin{array}{r} 3 \\ -\,2 \\ \hline \end{array}$ $\begin{array}{r} 10 \\ -\,9 \\ \hline \end{array}$ $\begin{array}{r} 5 \\ -\,2 \\ \hline \end{array}$ $\begin{array}{r} 7 \\ -\,5 \\ \hline \end{array}$ $\begin{array}{r} 4 \\ -\,3 \\ \hline \end{array}$

2. $\begin{array}{r} 9 \\ -\,6 \\ \hline \end{array}$ $\begin{array}{r} 8 \\ -\,7 \\ \hline \end{array}$ $\begin{array}{r} 6 \\ -\,4 \\ \hline \end{array}$ $\begin{array}{r} 7 \\ -\,4 \\ \hline \end{array}$ $\begin{array}{r} 5 \\ -\,4 \\ \hline \end{array}$ $\begin{array}{r} 8 \\ -\,5 \\ \hline \end{array}$

3. $\begin{array}{r} 5 \\ -\,3 \\ \hline \end{array}$ $\begin{array}{r} 8 \\ -\,6 \\ \hline \end{array}$ $\begin{array}{r} 9 \\ -\,8 \\ \hline \end{array}$ $\begin{array}{r} 6 \\ -\,5 \\ \hline \end{array}$ $\begin{array}{r} 10 \\ -\,7 \\ \hline \end{array}$ $\begin{array}{r} 9 \\ -\,7 \\ \hline \end{array}$

4. $\begin{array}{r} 6 \\ -\,3 \\ \hline \end{array}$ $\begin{array}{r} 7 \\ -\,6 \\ \hline \end{array}$ $\begin{array}{r} 10 \\ -\,8 \\ \hline \end{array}$ $\begin{array}{r} 4 \\ -\,2 \\ \hline \end{array}$ $\begin{array}{r} 5 \\ -\,3 \\ \hline \end{array}$ $\begin{array}{r} 9 \\ -\,6 \\ \hline \end{array}$

Reasoning

5. Solve.

Dan has 10 cards.

Dan has 1 more card than Becky.

Becky has 1 more card than Ted.

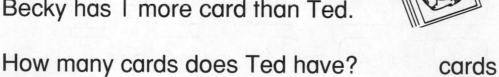

How many cards does Ted have? _____ cards

12

Fact Families

Write the fact families.

1.

7 (+) 3 (=) 10

___ ○ ___ ○ ___

___ ○ ___ ○ ___

___ ○ ___ ○ ___

2.

___ ○ ___ ○ ___

___ ○ ___ ○ ___

___ ○ ___ ○ ___

___ ○ ___ ○ ___

3.

___ ○ ___ ○ ___

___ ○ ___ ○ ___

___ ○ ___ ○ ___

___ ○ ___ ○ ___

4.

___ ○ ___ ○ ___

___ ○ ___ ○ ___

___ ○ ___ ○ ___

___ ○ ___ ○ ___

Number Sense

5. Look at the cube train. How
   many facts are in this family?_____

13

Problem-Solving Strategy
Write a Number Sentence

Write a number sentence to solve.

1. Helen had 9 pennies.
   She gave away 2 of them.
   How many did she have left?

$$\underline{9}\ \bigodot\ \underline{2}\ =\ \underline{7}$$

   $\underline{7}$ pennies

2. There are 4 roses.
   There are 6 tulips.
   How many flowers are there?

$$\underline{\quad}\ \bigcirc\ \underline{\quad}\ =\ \underline{\quad}$$

   _____ flowers

3. Lin buys 10 pears.
   She eats 4 of them.
   How many are left?

$$\underline{\quad}\ \bigcirc\ \underline{\quad}\ =\ \underline{\quad}$$

   _____ pears

Story Corner

4. Tell a story.
   Write a number sentence.

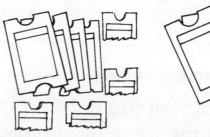

$$\underline{\quad}\ \bigcirc\ \underline{\quad}\ =\ \underline{\quad}$$

   _____ tickets

14

Doubles

Use counters.
Write the sums.

$$3 + 3 = 6$$

$$6 + 6 = 12$$

1.
$$1 + 1 = 2$$ $$7 + 7$$ $$2 + 2$$ $$8 + 8$$ $$4 + 4$$ $$5 + 5$$

2.
$$0 + 0$$ $$3 + 3$$ $$6 + 6$$ $$1 + 1$$ $$8 + 8$$ $$7 + 7$$

Write the sums. Then ring doubles.

3.
$$3 + 2$$ $$6 + 4$$ $$4 + 4$$ $$7 + 2$$ $$3 + 3$$ $$5 + 5$$

Problem Solving

4. Tony found 2 shells. David found the same number. How many shells did the boys find in all?

   _____ shells

5. Rosa saw 3 crabs in the sand. She saw the same number in the water. How many crabs did she see?

   _____ crabs

15

Doubles Plus One

Ring the numbers in each pair that have the greater sum. Then write the sums.

1. 4   (4)   3   3   6   5
   + 4   +5   + 4 + 3   + 5 + 5
    8   9

2. 6   6   2   2   8   9
   + 7   + 6   + 2 + 3   + 8 + 8

Add.

Ring sums of doubles 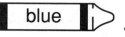 .

Ring sums of doubles plus one [yellow] .

3.   3   3   2   8   7   4
    +4   +3   +2   +7   +6   +4
     7

Visual Thinking

4. Ring the pictures that show doubles plus one.

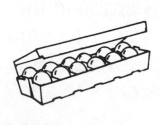   

Adding 9

Add.

1.

$$9 \atop {+5}$$
14
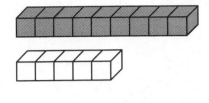

$$10 \atop {+4}$$
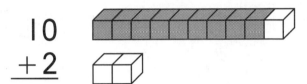

2.

$$9 \atop {+3}$$
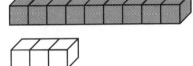

$$10 \atop {+2}$$

3.

$$9 \atop {+8}$$

$$10 \atop {+7}$$

4. $$9 \atop {+4}$$ (Think. 10 + 3) $$9 \atop {+6}$$ $$9 \atop {+7}$$ $$8 \atop {+9}$$ $$3 \atop {+9}$$

Number Sense

Ring the two that name the same number.

5. 9 + 2   10 + 3   10 + 1

6. 10 + 3   9 + 4   10 + 4

Make a 10

Use a 10-frame and counters.
Find the sums.

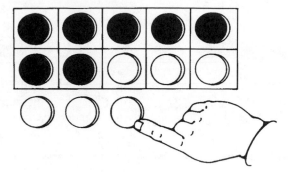

1.
$$\begin{array}{r} 7 \\ +6 \\ \hline 13 \end{array}$$
$$\begin{array}{r} 9 \\ +3 \\ \hline \end{array}$$
$$\begin{array}{r} 5 \\ +7 \\ \hline \end{array}$$
$$\begin{array}{r} 4 \\ +9 \\ \hline \end{array}$$
$$\begin{array}{r} 9 \\ +6 \\ \hline \end{array}$$
$$\begin{array}{r} 8 \\ +5 \\ \hline \end{array}$$

2.
$$\begin{array}{r} 2 \\ +9 \\ \hline \end{array}$$
$$\begin{array}{r} 8 \\ +6 \\ \hline \end{array}$$
$$\begin{array}{r} 9 \\ +5 \\ \hline \end{array}$$
$$\begin{array}{r} 6 \\ +9 \\ \hline \end{array}$$
$$\begin{array}{r} 4 \\ +7 \\ \hline \end{array}$$
$$\begin{array}{r} 9 \\ +4 \\ \hline \end{array}$$

3.
$$\begin{array}{r} 3 \\ +8 \\ \hline \end{array}$$
$$\begin{array}{r} 8 \\ +4 \\ \hline \end{array}$$
$$\begin{array}{r} 7 \\ +5 \\ \hline \end{array}$$
$$\begin{array}{r} 9 \\ +7 \\ \hline \end{array}$$
$$\begin{array}{r} 6 \\ +8 \\ \hline \end{array}$$
$$\begin{array}{r} 5 \\ +9 \\ \hline \end{array}$$

Problem Solving

Write a number sentence to solve.

4. Miko saw 7 seals. Soon 5 of them swam away. How many seals were left?

_____ ⃝ _____ = _____

_____ seals

5. Alice saw 6 baby seals and 7 mother seals. How many seals did she see?

_____ ⃝ _____ = _____

_____ seals

Adding More Than Two Addends

Sometimes, looking for a 10 or a double
makes adding easy.
Add.

1.
$$\left.\begin{array}{r} 2 \\ 2 \end{array}\right\}4$$
$$+7$$
¦ ¦

$$\left.\begin{array}{r} 2 \\ 6 \end{array}\right\}10$$
$$+4$$

$$\left.\begin{array}{r} 5 \\ 3 \end{array}\right\}6$$
$$+3$$

$$\left.\begin{array}{r} 4 \\ 4 \end{array}\right\}8$$
$$+5$$

$$\left.\begin{array}{r} 8 \\ 2 \end{array}\right\}10$$
$$\begin{array}{r} 1 \\ +3 \end{array}$$

2.
$$\begin{array}{r} 7 \\ 5 \\ +5 \end{array}$$
$$\begin{array}{r} 8 \\ 2 \\ +7 \end{array}$$
$$\begin{array}{r} 1 \\ 4 \\ 6 \\ +3 \end{array}$$
$$\begin{array}{r} 1 \\ 8 \\ 4 \\ +4 \end{array}$$
$$\begin{array}{r} 6 \\ 4 \\ 3 \\ +2 \end{array}$$
$$\begin{array}{r} 3 \\ 3 \\ 6 \\ +1 \end{array}$$

3.
$$\begin{array}{r} 6 \\ 3 \\ +7 \end{array}$$
$$\begin{array}{r} 2 \\ 1 \\ 6 \\ +6 \end{array}$$
$$\begin{array}{r} 4 \\ 5 \\ 5 \\ +2 \end{array}$$
$$\begin{array}{r} 9 \\ 0 \\ 9 \\ +1 \end{array}$$
$$\begin{array}{r} 0 \\ 8 \\ 2 \\ +8 \end{array}$$
$$\begin{array}{r} 2 \\ 2 \\ 4 \\ +6 \end{array}$$

Reasoning

Do these in your head.
Ring the ones with a sum greater than 10.

4. 4 + 1 + 1 + 1 + 6   5. 2 + 1 + 1 + 2 + 1

6. 1 + 1 + 1 + 3 + 7   7. 5 + 1 + 1 + 5

8. 1 + 1 + 1 + 1 + 1 + 1 + 1 + 1

19

Sums to 14

Complete the addition sentences.

1. | 14 |

$5 +$ __9__ $=$ __14__

$6 +$ _____ $=$ _____

$7 +$ _____ $=$ _____

_____ $+$ _____ $=$ _____

2. | 13 |

$4 +$ _____ $=$ _____

$5 +$ _____ $=$ _____

$6 +$ _____ $=$ _____

_____ $+$ _____ $=$ _____

3. | 12 |

$3 +$ _____ $=$ _____

$4 +$ _____ $=$ _____

$5 +$ _____ $=$ _____

_____ $+$ _____ $=$ _____

4. | 11 |

$2 +$ _____ $=$ _____

$3 +$ _____ $=$ _____

$4 +$ _____ $=$ _____

_____ $+$ _____ $=$ _____

Reasoning

5. Continue the pattern. Write a number name on each of the last two  .

$7+7$ $6+7$ $5+7$ $4+7$

20

Problem Solving

Choose the Operation

Read each story.
Then write the number sentence to solve.

1. There are 5 young dolphins. There are 5 older dolphins. How many dolphins are there altogether?

   $\underline{5}$ $\bigoplus$ $\underline{5}$ $=$ $\underline{10}$

2. A dolphin has 8 rings. A seal has 6 rings. How many more rings does the dolphin have than the seal?

   $\underline{}$ $\bigcirc$ $\underline{}$ $=$ $\underline{}$

3. There are 11 seals on a rock. Then 2 of them dive. How many are left?

   $\underline{}$ $\bigcirc$ $\underline{}$ $=$ $\underline{}$

4. A seal eats 5 small fish. Then the seal eats 7 more. How many fish does the seal eat?

   $\underline{}$ $\bigcirc$ $\underline{}$ $=$ $\underline{}$

Story Corner

5. Tell a story about the picture. Write a number sentence.

   $\underline{}$ $\bigcirc$ $\underline{}$ $=$ $\underline{}$

Sums to 18

Add.

1.
$$\begin{array}{r} 8 \\ +5 \\ \hline 13 \end{array}$$
$$\begin{array}{r} 7 \\ +7 \\ \hline \end{array}$$
$$\begin{array}{r} 5 \\ +7 \\ \hline \end{array}$$
$$\begin{array}{r} 9 \\ +4 \\ \hline \end{array}$$
$$\begin{array}{r} 9 \\ +8 \\ \hline \end{array}$$
$$\begin{array}{r} 6 \\ +6 \\ \hline \end{array}$$

2.
$$\begin{array}{r} 6 \\ +8 \\ \hline \end{array}$$
$$\begin{array}{r} 4 \\ +7 \\ \hline \end{array}$$
$$\begin{array}{r} 6 \\ +8 \\ \hline \end{array}$$
$$\begin{array}{r} 5 \\ +9 \\ \hline \end{array}$$
$$\begin{array}{r} 6 \\ +9 \\ \hline \end{array}$$
$$\begin{array}{r} 7 \\ +6 \\ \hline \end{array}$$

3.
$$\begin{array}{r} 9 \\ +3 \\ \hline \end{array}$$
$$\begin{array}{r} 9 \\ +9 \\ \hline \end{array}$$
$$\begin{array}{r} 7 \\ +4 \\ \hline \end{array}$$
$$\begin{array}{r} 6 \\ +7 \\ \hline \end{array}$$
$$\begin{array}{r} 8 \\ +8 \\ \hline \end{array}$$
$$\begin{array}{r} 4 \\ +8 \\ \hline \end{array}$$

4.
$$\begin{array}{r} 9 \\ +8 \\ \hline \end{array}$$
$$\begin{array}{r} 2 \\ +9 \\ \hline \end{array}$$
$$\begin{array}{r} 3 \\ +9 \\ \hline \end{array}$$
$$\begin{array}{r} 6 \\ +5 \\ \hline \end{array}$$
$$\begin{array}{r} 7 \\ +5 \\ \hline \end{array}$$
$$\begin{array}{r} 5 \\ +6 \\ \hline \end{array}$$

Problem Solving

Write a number sentence. Solve.

5. There were 11 birds in the air. Then 8 of the birds landed. How many birds were still in the air?

_____ ◯ _____ = _____

_____ birds

6. There were 5 pink birds and 8 white birds standing in the water. How many birds were in the water?

_____ ◯ _____ = _____

_____ birds

Using Doubles to Subtract

Add or subtract.
Then match.

1. $6 + 6 =$ __12__

2. $5 + 5 =$ ___

3. $9 + 9 =$ ___

4. $2 + 2 =$ ___

5. $3 + 3 =$ ___

6. $7 + 7 =$ ___

7. $4 + 4 =$ ___

8. $8 + 8 =$ ___

$10 - 5 =$ ___

$4 - 2 =$ ___

$12 - 6 =$ __6__

$14 - 7 =$ ___

$6 - 3 =$ ___

$18 - 9 =$ ___

$16 - 8 =$ ___

$8 - 4 =$ ___

Problem Solving

9. Leo put 6 orange fish and 6 black fish in the bowl. How many fish did Leo put in?

____ ◯ ____ = ____

____ fish

10. Leo had 12 fish in his bowl. Then he took out 6 fish to put in his tank. How many fish were left in the bowl?

____ ◯ ____ = ____

____ fish

Using Other Addition Facts to Subtract

Subtract. Then color.

Color Code

Answer	Color
2	black
3	purple
4	blue
5	brown
6	yellow
7	red
8	green
9	orange

Number Sense

Do these in your head. Then write
the sums and differences.

1. 9 + 4 = 13,
   so 13 − 4 = _____ .

2. 13 − 9 = 4,
   so 4 + 9 = _____ .

3. 6 + 7 = 13,
   so 13 − 7 = _____ .

4. 13 − 6 = 7,
   so 7 + 6 = _____ .

Related Addition and Subtraction Facts

Write the differences.

1.

Subtract 3.	
12	9
10	
11	

Subtract 5.	
11	
14	
13	

Subtract 4.	
11	
13	
12	

Subtract 6.	
14	
12	
8	

2.

Subtract 8.	
16	
12	
14	

Subtract 9.	
10	
15	
18	

Subtract 7.	
13	
16	
9	

Subtract 5.	
14	
11	
13	

3.

Subtract 6.	
10	
15	
9	

Subtract 8.	
13	
11	
15	

Subtract 9.	
11	
17	
16	

Subtract 7.	
15	
14	
10	

Problem Solving

Write a number sentence to solve.

4. There were 6 snails on the rock. There were 7 snails in the sand. How many snails were there?

____ ◯ ____ = ____

_____ snails

5. Rico had 12 shells, but he gave 3 away. How many shells did he have left?

____ ◯ ____ = ____

_____ shells

Fact Families

Complete each number sentence.
Which one does not belong to
the fact family? Ring it.

1. 15 − _7_ = 8

   7 + 8 = ___

   7 + 7 = ___

   ___ − 8 = 7

   ___ + 7 = 15

2. 7 + 9 = ___

   ___ − 9 = 7

   16 − ___ = 9

   9 + ___ = 16

   9 + 9 = ___

3. 9 + ___ = 17

   8 + ___ = 17

   ___ − 9 = 8

   17 − 8 = ___

   16 − 8 = ___

4. 15 − 9 = ___

   14 − 8 = ___

   6 + ___ = 14

   ___ − 6 = 8

   8 + 6 = ___

Number Sense

5. Write the fact family for ⛃⛃⛃⛃⛃⛃ ⛃⛃⛃⛃⛃⛃.

   ___ + ___ = ___   ___ − ___ = ___

Using Addition and Subtraction

Add or subtract.
Use your addition table if you need to.

1. $9 + 7 =$ __16__ $16 - 7 =$ ___ $7 + 9 =$ ___

2. $5 + 8 =$ ___ $13 - 8 =$ ___ $8 + 5 =$ ___

3. $6 + 5 =$ ___ $11 - 5 =$ ___ $5 + 6 =$ ___

4.
$$
\begin{array}{cccccc}
7 & 18 & 4 & 9 & 11 & 14 \\
+7 & -9 & +7 & +9 & -4 & -7 \\
\end{array}
$$

5.
$$
\begin{array}{cccccc}
15 & 12 & 8 & 7 & 13 & 4 \\
-7 & -4 & +5 & +8 & -8 & +8 \\
\end{array}
$$

Problem Solving

Read each story.
Then write the number sentence to solve.

6. There were 5 red pails and 5 yellow pails in the shop. How many pails were there?

___ ◯ ___ = ___

____ pails

7. There were 5 red beach balls and 6 yellow balls in the shop. How many balls were there?

___ ◯ ___ = ___

____ balls

Problem Solving
Too Much Information

Draw a line through
the sentence that is not needed.
Then write a number sentence to solve.

1. Carolyn has 12 sea
plants. ~~Josh has 6 sea plants.~~ Carolyn gives
Jim 5 plants. How
many plants does she
have left?

$$\underline{12} \bigodot \underline{5} = \underline{7}$$

__7__ plants

2. Kara buys 2 nets for
fishing. She has 8 other
nets. Kara has 4 fishing
poles. How many nets
does Kara have?

____ ⃝ ____ = ____

____ nets

3. There are 9 men
fishing. There are 8
women fishing. There
are 12 boats. How
many people are
fishing?

____ ⃝ ____ = ____

____ people

4. Marta has 11 clams.
Yesterday Marta found
4 crabs. Marta has 6
fish. How many more
clams does she have
than fish?

____ ⃝ ____ = ____

____ more clams

Story Corner

5. Tell a story about the
picture. Write a number
sentence.

____ ⃝ ____ = ____

Grouping Tens

Complete the table.

How many tens? How many in all?

		How many tens?	How many in all?
1.		__1__ ten	__10__ stickers in all
2.		_____ tens	_____ stickers in all
3.		_____ tens	_____ stickers in all
4.		_____ tens	_____ stickers in all
5.		_____ tens	_____ stickers in all
6.		_____ tens	_____ stickers in all

Number Sense

Which is the greater number? Ring it.

7.   30   7 tens   8.   4 tens   50

Tens and Ones

Ring groups of ten.
Write how many tens and ones.
Then write how many in all.

1.

__2__ tens __3__ ones __23__

2.

___ tens ___ ones ___

3.

___ tens ___ ones ___

4.

___ tens ___ one ___

5.

___ tens ___ one ___

6.

___ tens ___ ones ___

Visual Thinking

7. Which is easier to count? Ring it. Tell why.

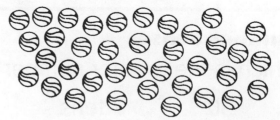

Tens and Ones to 50

Write the numbers.

1. 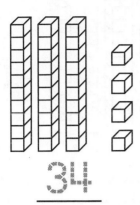 34 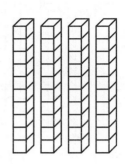 _____ _____

Use tens and ones.
Ring the number.

2. 3 tens   2 ones   1 ten   4 ones   4 ones

   32   23   41   14   40   4

---

3. 2 tens   1 one   2 tens   4 ones   3 tens

   21   12   42   24   30   3

Number Sense

Write the mystery numbers.

4. Emily's mystery number has a 2 in the tens place and a 5 in the ones place.

5. Alonzo's mystery number has a 7 in the tens place and a 4 in the ones place.

   _____   _____

Tens and Ones to 100

Write the numbers.

1.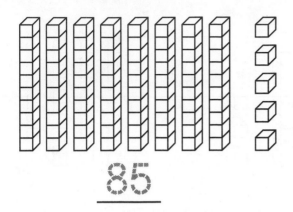

85
_____   _____

---

2. 8 tens   7 ones   _____   **3.** 6 tens   3 ones   _____

4. 5 tens   9 ones   _____   **5.** 8 tens   6 ones   _____

Ring the number.

6. 9 tens   2 ones   6 tens   5 ones   8 ones   3 tens

    92   29   65   56   38   83

---

7. 7 tens   6 ones   4 ones   8 tens   9 ones   3 tens

    67   76   48   84   39   93

Visual Thinking

8.

Ring the better estimate.

66

more than 30   fewer than 30

32

Exchanging Dimes for Pennies

Match.

1.

2.

3.

4.

Number Sense

5. Ring the greater amount of money.

Ordering Numbers to 100

Write the month and the year.
Complete the calendar for next month.

_____

Sunday	Monday	Tuesday	Wednesday	Thursday	Friday	Saturday

Write the answers.

1. How many Fridays are in next month?   _____

2. How many days are in next month?   _____

Reasoning

3. Ring the numbers that end in 5 or 0.
   What skip-counting pattern do you see? Ring it.

1	2	3	4	5	6	7	8	9	10
11	12	13	14	15	16	17	18	19	20

counting by twos   counting by fives   counting by tens

34

After, Before, Between

Write each hidden number.

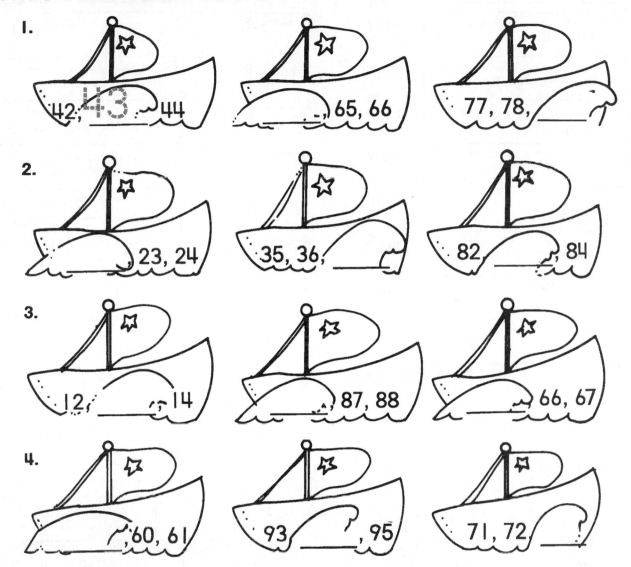

1. 42, _43_, 44   ___, 65, 66   77, 78, ___

2. ___, 23, 24   35, 36, ___   82, ___, 84

3. 12, ___, 14   ___, 87, 88   ___, 66, 67

4. ___, 60, 61   93, ___, 95   71, 72, ___

Reasoning

Write the missing number.
Look for a pattern.

5. 62, 64, 66, 68, 70, 72, _____

6. _____, 30, 40, 50, 60, 70

7. 51, 53, _____, 57, 59

Ordinal Numbers

1. Color the floors.

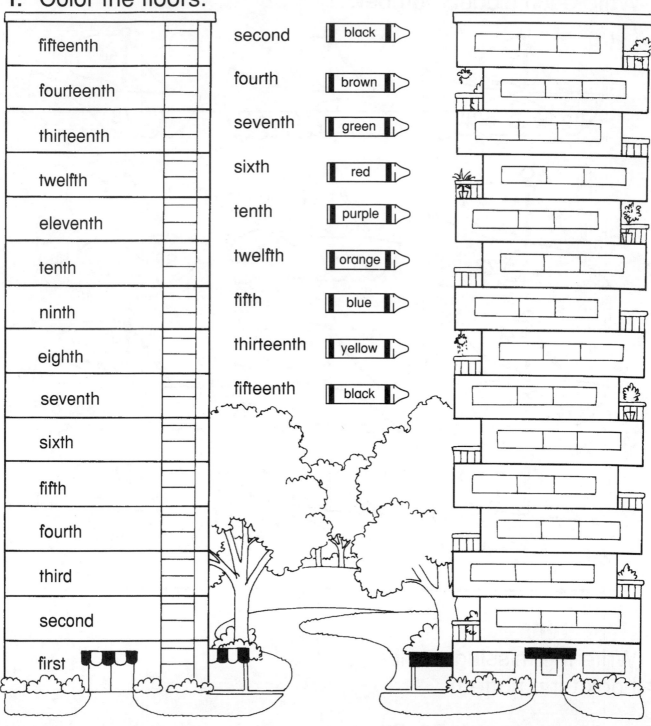

fifteenth	
fourteenth	
thirteenth	
twelfth	
eleventh	
tenth	
ninth	
eighth	
seventh	
sixth	
fifth	
fourth	
third	
second	
first	

second — black

fourth — brown

seventh — green

sixth — red

tenth — purple

twelfth — orange

fifth — blue

thirteenth — yellow

fifteenth — black

Number Sense

Ring the word for the higher floor.

2. ninth   fourth

3. fifteenth   twelfth

36

Number Patterns

Complete the table.
Write the missing numbers.

1	⟨2⟩	⟨3⟩	4	5	6	7	8	9	10
11			14	15	16	17	18	19	20
21			24	25	26	27	28	29	30
31			34	35	36	37	38	39	40
41			44	45	46	47	48	49	50
51			54	55	56	57	58	59	60
61			64	65	66	67	68	69	70
71			74	75	76	77	78	79	80
81			84	85	86	87	88	89	90
91			94	95	96	97	98	99	100

1. Count by threes to 30. Ring the numbers [purple ▷] .
2. Count by twos to 30. Ring the numbers [green ▷] .

Reasoning

3. Continue the pattern.

   1, 11, 21, 31, 41, _____, _____

Problem Solving

Extend and Create Patterns

Look for a pattern.
Write the missing numbers.

1. 85, 75, 65, _____, _____, 35, _____, _____, 5

2. 1, 5, 9, 13, _____, _____, _____, _____, 33

3. 49, 47, 45, 43, 41, _____, _____, 35, _____, _____

4. 2, 5, 8, 11, _____, _____, _____, _____, _____

5. 24, 34, 44, _____, _____, _____, _____, _____

Story Corner

Tell a friend about the patterns.

6.

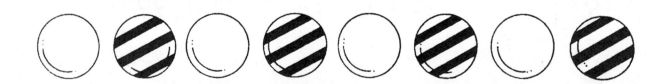

7.

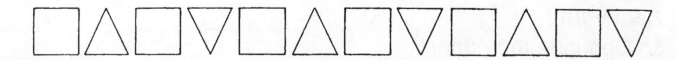

38

Even and Odd Numbers

Use cubes. Then color to show each number.
Ring even numbers in red.
Ring odd numbers in blue.

If no cubes are left over, the number is even. If I cube is left over, the number is odd.

1. (4) red

2. 7

3. I

4. 8

5. 5

6. 2

7. Use cubes.
Ring the even numbers in red.
Ring the odd numbers in blue.

3   7   32   25   6   48   13   41   22

Problem Solving

Add any two even numbers to solve.
Ring the answer.

8. Even Number + Even Number = ?   Even Number

Odd Number

Comparing Numbers

Write each number. Then
ring the greater number.

1.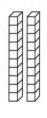

_(15)_   _12_

_____   _____

2.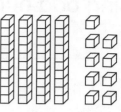

_____   _____

Write each number. Ring the
number that is less.

3.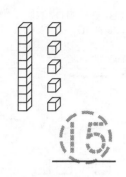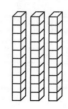

_____   _____

4.

_____   _____

5.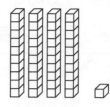

_____   _____

6.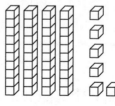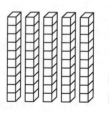

_____   _____

Problem Solving

Write the number.

7. I am 3 greater than 72.
I am 1 less than 76.

_____

8. I am 5 greater than 61.
I am 3 less than 69.

_____

Greater Than and Less Than

Use place-value models to show each
pair of numbers.
Then write < or > in each circle.

1. 56 (>) 54   36 ( ) 37   35 ( ) 52

2. 57 ( ) 45   24 ( ) 21   48 ( ) 60

3. 12 ( ) 14   8 ( ) 11   7 ( ) 4

4. 22 ( ) 12   41 ( ) 61   40 ( ) 30

Write your own number sentences.

5. _____ > 64   _____ < 33   17 < _____

6. 29 ( ) _____   _____ ( ) 48   30 ( ) _____

Reasoning

7. Write a number that comes before 75.

   _____

8. Write a number that comes after 75.

   _____

9. Which of the two numbers is greater?

   Write it. _____

Problem-Solving Strategy

Make a Table

Complete the table to find a pattern.

1. Tyrone has a coin collection.
   He puts 5 coins in each box.
   How many coins
   are in 4 boxes?   _____ coins

	1	2	3	
	5	10		

2. Each coin costs 4¢.
   Tyrone spent 24¢.
   How many coins
   did he buy?   _____ coins

	1	2	3			
	4	8	12			

Reasoning

3. How many coins can
   Tyrone put in 6 boxes?   _____ coins

Counting Patterns

You need a 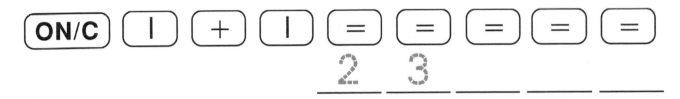 .

Use your calculator. Finish the counting patterns. Write each number you see.

1. Press

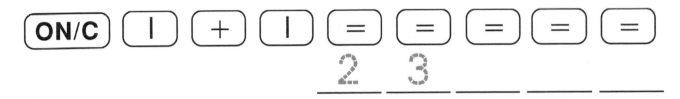

ON/C 1 + 1 = = = = =

2 3 ___ ___ ___ ___ ___

2. Press

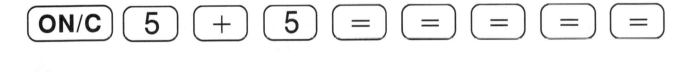

ON/C 5 + 5 = = = = =

___ ___ ___ ___ ___ ___

3. Press

ON/C 2 5 + 5 = = = =

___ ___ ___ ___

Reasoning

4. How can you get your calculator to count by threes?

_____

Counting Pennies, Nickels, and Dimes

Count on to find the total amount.

1.

_5_ ¢ _10_ ¢ _15_ ¢ _16_ ¢ | 16 | ¢

2.

____ ¢ ____ ¢ ____ ¢ ____ ¢   ¢

3.

____ ¢ ____ ¢ ____ ¢ ____ ¢ ____ ¢   ¢

4.

____ ¢ ____ ¢ ____ ¢ ____ ¢ ____ ¢ ____ ¢   ¢

Number Sense

Use punch-out coins.
Trace and write the value on each coin.

5. Use 3 coins to show 15¢.   **6.** Use 4 coins to show 40¢.

44

Quarter

Count on from 25¢.
Write the total amount.

1.

   __25__ ¢ __35__ ¢ __40__ ¢ __41__ ¢ | 41 | ¢

2.

   _____ ¢ _____ ¢ _____ ¢ _____ ¢ _____ ¢ | | ¢

3.

   _____ ¢ _____ ¢ _____ ¢ _____ ¢ _____ ¢ | | ¢

4.

   _____ ¢ _____ ¢ _____ ¢ _____ ¢ _____ ¢ _____ ¢ | | ¢

Problem Solving

Use punch-out coins. Solve.

5. Phil has 1 quarter, 2 nickels, and 1 penny. How much money does Phil have?

   _____ ¢

6. Anna has 2 nickels. Sam has 3 pennies. How much more money does Anna have?

   _____ ¢ more

45

Comparing Money

Greatest Amount

Count on to find the total amounts.
Ring the greatest amount.

1.

_31_ ¢   _25_ ¢   (36) ¢

2.

_____ ¢   _____ ¢   _____ ¢

3.

_____ ¢   _____ ¢   _____ ¢

Reasoning

4. Len has 24¢.
    Tina has 44¢.
    Who can buy the toy?

_____

Half Dollar

Which children can buy the book?
Write the amounts.
Then ring the names.

1. (Nancy)

50 ¢
_____

2. Edith

45 ¢
_____

3. Glen

_____ ¢

4. Alan

_____ ¢

5. Rita

_____ ¢

6. David

_____ ¢

Visual Thinking

7. Look carefully at a nickel.
   Put it away.
   Picture it in your mind.
   Describe it to a friend.
   Have your friend guess the coin.

It is bigger than a penny.
It is . . . .

Problem-Solving Strategy
Make a Model

Write the amounts.

1. Robert has I quarter, I dime, and 2 pennies. He spends I dime. How much money does he have now?

   _27_ ¢

2. Nema has 5 nickels and 3 pennies. She spends 3 nickels. How much money does she have now?

   ____ ¢

3. Julia has 2 dimes, 2 nickels, and 2 pennies. She spends I dime and I nickel. How much money does she have left?

   ____ ¢

4. Greg has I quarter, I nickel, and 5 pennies. He finds 5 pennies. How much money does he have?

   ____ ¢

5. Harry has 6 nickels and I penny. He gives 3 nickels to a friend. How much money does he have now?

   ____ ¢

6. Mae has I quarter and 4 nickels. She finds I dime. How much money does Mae have?

   ____ ¢

Story Corner

7. Look at the pictures. Make up a money story. Share it with a friend.

48

Counting On from 50¢

Count on. Write the total amount.

1.

   50¢   75¢   80¢   85¢   [85]¢

2.

   ___¢   ___¢   ___¢   ___¢   [ ]¢

3.

   ___¢   ___¢   ___¢   ___¢   [ ]¢

4.

   ___¢   ___¢   ___¢   ___¢   ___¢   [ ]¢

Visual Thinking

5. Tran has 58¢ in all.
   What coins are left in her bank?
   Write how many.
   Ring the coin name.

   _____   dimes   nickels   pennies

49

Combinations of Coins

Count on to find out how much money.
Write the total amount.

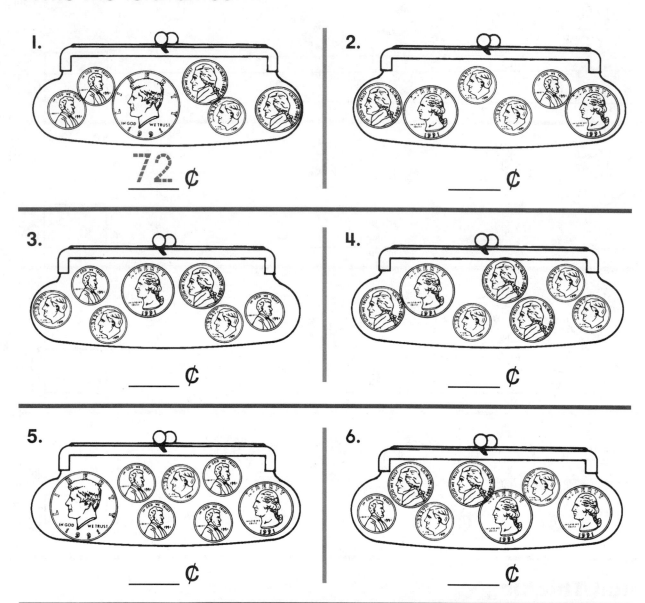

1. 72 ¢

2. _____ ¢

3. _____ ¢

4. _____ ¢

5. _____ ¢

6. _____ ¢

Reasoning

7. John has 67¢.
   Ring the belt that he can buy.

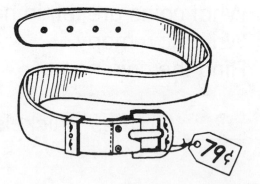

59¢

79¢

Equal Amounts

Work with a friend.
Use your punch-out coins.
Write the amount.
Work together to find fewer coins to
make the same amount. Draw.
Write the value on each coin.

I.

_55_ ¢

2.

_____ ¢

3.

_____ ¢

Number Sense

4. Which amount could you make with
   the fewest coins? Use punch-out
   coins. Ring the amount.   41¢   51¢   61¢

Counting Change

Work with a friend.
Count up from the price to find the change.
Use punch-out coins to count out the
change to your friend.

1. You have 70¢.
You buy

 58¢

59¢ _60_ ¢ _70_ ¢

You have _12_ ¢ change.

---

2. You have 45¢.
You buy

 38¢

39¢ _____ ¢ _____ ¢

You have _____ ¢ change.

---

3. You have 65¢.
You buy

 52¢

53 ¢ _____ ¢ _____ ¢ _____ ¢

You have _____ ¢ change.

Number Sense

Solve. Use punch-out coins.
Trace and write the value on each coin.

4. Janine has 50¢ to spend.
   She buys a pin for 24¢.
   Use the fewest coins possible to show Janine's change.

Problem Solving

Make a Decision

Do you have enough money?
Write the amount. Then ring **Yes** or **No**.

1. You have   . 95 ¢

Do you have enough money to buy a ? (Yes) No

2. You have   . _____ ¢

Do you have enough money to buy a  ? Yes No

3. You have    . _____ ¢

Do you have enough money to buy a  ? Yes No

4. You have   . _____ ¢

Do you have enough money to buy a  ? Yes No

Number Sense

5. Ring the better estimate.

more than 50¢

less than 50¢

Hour

Draw the hour hand so that both clocks show the same time.

1.

Draw the minute hand so that both clocks show the same time.

2.

Draw the hour hand and the minute hand.

3.

Reasoning

Ring the reasonable answer.

4. Maria eats dinner at _____ .   3:00   6:00

54

Understanding Time

Hour

Read the time.
Use a punch-out clock.
Show 1 hour later. Then draw hands on
the clock to show 1 hour later.

1. `4:00`

2. `9:00`

3. `1:00`

4. `10:00`

5. `5:00`

6. `11:00`

Problem Solving

Solve. Write the answer.

7. The bus leaves in 1 hour.
   It is 2:00 now. What time will the bus leave? _____ : _____

30 Minutes

Half Hour

Write the times.

1.

| 9:30 | : | : |

2.

| : | : | : |

3.

| : | : | : |

Problem Solving

Solve. Write the answer.

4. The bus comes at 8:00.
It takes 30 minutes to get to school.
What time will the bus get there? ____:____

15 Minutes

Quarter Hour

Write the times.

1.

5:15   :   :

2.

:   :   :

3.

:   :   :

Problem Solving

Use a punch-out clock. Write the times.

4. It is 8:30.
   What time will it be
   in 15 minutes? ___ : ___

5. It is 2:15.
   What time will it be
   in 15 minutes? ___ : ___

Problem Solving

Use Data

9:00–9:30	9:30–10:30	10:30–12:30	12:30–1:00	1:00–1:30	1:30–2:00	2:00–3:00
Breakfast	Music	Hiking	Lunch	Crafts	Sailing	Swimming

This is Paul's schedule for one day at camp. Read the schedule. Write the answers.

1. When does hiking begin?

   10:30

2. When does hiking end?

   ___:___

3. How long is hiking?

   _____ hours

4. How many minutes pass from the beginning of breakfast until the beginning of music?

   _____ minutes

5. How long is sailing?

   _____ minutes

6. How long is music?

   _____ hour

Number Sense

Ring the better estimate.

7. Paul swims from 2:00 to 3:15.

   He swims for about _____.   a half hour   an hour

58

Minutes

Write the times.

1.

8:15   __:__   __:__   __:__

2.

__:__   __:__   __:__   __:__

3.

__:__   __:__   __:__   __:__

Number Sense

Ring the better answer.

4. Dee jogs until 4:20.
   It is almost _____.

   4:00   4:30

5. Angie swims until 4:55.
   It is almost _____.

   4:30   5:00

Estimating Time

About how long will it take?
Ring the better estimate.

1.

I minute
I hour

to wash hands

2.

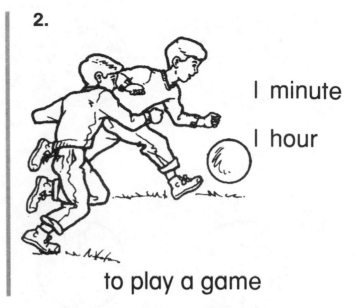

I minute

I hour

to play a game

3.

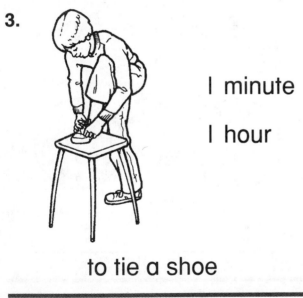

I minute

I hour

to tie a shoe

4.

I minute

I hour

to fix dinner

Story Corner

Ring the correct word to complete each sentence.

5. I take a few _____ to brush my teeth.   minutes   hours

6. I spend two or three _____ at the movies. minutes   hours

Using the Calendar

Calendar

January
S	M	T	W	T	F	S
			1	2	3	4
5	6	7	8	9	10	11
12	13	14	15	16	17	18
19	20	21	22	23	24	25
26	27	28	29	30	31	

February
S	M	T	W	T	F	S
						1 8 15 22 29
2	3	4	5	6	7	
9	10	11	12	13	14	
16	17	18	19	20	21	
23	24	25	26	37	28	

March
S	M	T	W	T	F	S
1	2	3	4	5	6	7
8	9	10	11	12	13	14
15	16	17	18	19	20	21
22	23	24	25	26	27	28
29	30	31				

April
S	M	T	W	T	F	S
			1	2	3	4
5	6	7	8	9	10	11
12	13	14	15	16	17	18
19	20	21	22	23	24	25
26	27	28	29	30		

May
S	M	T	W	T	F	S
					1	2
3	4	5	6	7	8	9
10	11	12	13	14	15	16
17	18	19	20	21	22	23
24/31	25	26	27	28	29	30

June
S	M	T	W	T	F	S
	1	2	3	4	5	6
7	8	9	10	11	12	13
14	15	16	17	18	19	20
21	22	23	24	25	26	27
28	29	30				

July
S	M	T	W	T	F	S
			1	2	3	4
5	6	7	8	9	10	11
12	13	14	15	16	17	18
19	20	21	22	23	24	25
26	27	28	29	30	31	

August
S	M	T	W	T	F	S
						1
2	3	4	5	6	7	8
9	10	11	12	13	14	15
16	17	18	19	20	21	22
23/30	24/31	25	26	27	28	29

September
S	M	T	W	T	F	S
		1	2	3	4	5
6	7	8	9	10	11	12
13	14	15	16	17	18	19
20	21	22	23	24	25	26
27	28	29	30			

October
S	M	T	W	T	F	S
				1	2	3
4	5	6	7	8	9	10
11	12	13	14	15	16	17
18	19	20	21	22	23	24
25	26	27	28	29	30	31

November
S	M	T	W	T	F	S
1	2	3	4	5	6	7
8	9	10	11	12	13	14
15	16	17	18	19	20	21
22	23	24	25	26	27	28
29	30					

December
S	M	T	W	T	F	S
		1	2	3	4	5
6	7	8	9	10	11	12
13	14	15	16	17	18	19
20	21	22	23	24	25	26
27	28	29	30	31		

Ring these special dates on the calendar.
1. the first day of June
2. the last day of September
3. Thanksgiving Day, November 26
4. Independence Day, July 4
5. Valentine's Day, February 14
6. Mother's Day, May 10
7. Father's Day, June 21
8. April Fools' Day, April 1

Reasoning

9. Paula's birthday is 7 days before Peter's birthday. Paula's birthday is on Friday. On what day is Peter's birthday?

Problem-Solving Strategy

Draw a Picture

The magic hen will lay 1 egg every 5 minutes.
Draw the eggs that will be in the nest
at each time.

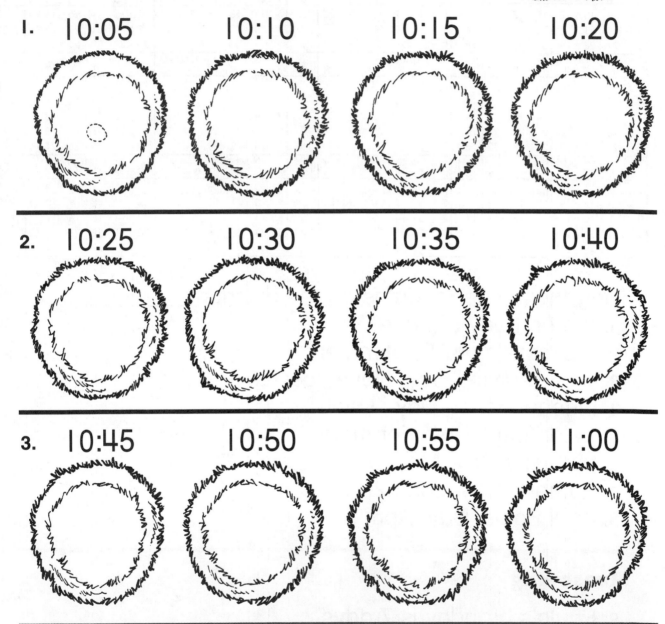

1. 10:05   10:10   10:15   10:20

2. 10:25   10:30   10:35   10:40

3. 10:45   10:50   10:55   11:00

Visual Thinking

4. Ring the ice cubes that have been
   in the glass for 30 minutes.

Understanding Regrouping

Work with a friend.
Complete the table.

	Ones	Join. Write how many.	Can you make a ten? Ring Yes or No.	Trade. Write how many.
1.	8 7	_15_ ones	(Yes) No	_1_ ten _5_ ones
2.	4 5	___ ones	Yes No	___ ten ___ ones
3.	9 4	___ ones	Yes No	___ ten ___ ones
4.	6 6	___ ones	Yes No	___ ten ___ ones

Number Sense

5. Ring the two that name the same number.

I ten 3 ones   II ones   13 ones   I ten 0 ones

More Regrouping

Put in tens and ones to show each problem.

Complete the table.

	Show	Join the ones. Write how many.	Can you make a ten? Ring Yes or No.		Trade. Write how many.
1.	13 + 8	11 ones	(Yes)	No	2 tens 1 ones
2.	35 + 7	___ ones	Yes	No	___ tens ___ ones
3.	68 + 1	___ ones	Yes	No	___ tens ___ ones
4.	29 + 9	___ ones	Yes	No	___ tens ___ ones
5.	46 + 7	___ ones	Yes	No	___ tens ___ ones

Visual Thinking

6. Write how many.

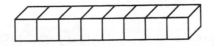

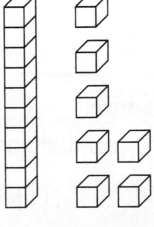

_____ cubes   _____ cubes

Understanding 2-Digit Addition

Add. Trade if you need to.

1.
tens	ones
2	5
+	8
3	3

tens	ones
4	3
+	7

tens	ones
2	1
+	2

tens	ones
2	8
+	2

2.
tens	ones
2	9
+	2

tens	ones
5	6
+	6

tens	ones
2	3
+	8

tens	ones
6	5
+	9

3.
tens	ones
4	5
+	8

tens	ones
3	3
+	9

tens	ones
5	7
+	5

tens	ones
3	0
+	4

Number Sense

Ring the better estimate.

4. 50 + 30 = 80, so 42 + 28 is 　　greater than 80.
　　　　　　　　　　　　　　　　　　less than 80.

5. 50 + 30 = 80, so 50 + 35 is 　　greater than 80.
　　　　　　　　　　　　　　　　　　less than 80.

Adding 2-Digit Numbers

Add. Trade if you need to.

1.

tens	ones
1	
4	2
+ 1	9
6	1

tens	ones
2	9
+ 1	7

tens	ones
4	7
+ 2	9

tens	ones
5	8
+ 1	6

2.

tens	ones
2	7
+ 1	2

tens	ones
1	9
+ 3	2

tens	ones
	5
+ 4	8

tens	ones
2	2
+ 3	8

Problem Solving

Solve.

3. Cal had 29 cubes. His uncle gave him 15 cubes for his birthday. Then how many cubes did Cal have?

4. Wendy had 4 tens and 2 ones. Then she got 3 more tens and 9 more ones. She traded ones for a ten. Then how many tens and ones did she have?

_____ cubes   _____ tens and _____ ones

More Adding 2-Digit Numbers

Find the sum.

1.
```
  38      55      23      29      24      19
+ 38    + 21    +45     +44     +47    + 28
  76
```

2.
```
  84      82      12      37      78      54
+ 15    + 14    +28     + 25    + 19    + 27
```

3.
```
  68      67      19      26      73      86
+  8    + 13    +  3    + 19    + 10    +  7
```

Problem Solving

Ring the answer.

4. Theo had 5 tens and 15 ones. He traded 10 ones for a ten. Shari had 5 tens and 12 ones. She traded 10 ones for a ten. After that, who had more ones, Theo or Shari?

Theo   Shari

Addition Practice

Add.

1.
$$
\begin{array}{r} 19 \\ + 28 \\ \hline \end{array}
\qquad
\begin{array}{r} 57 \\ + 26 \\ \hline \end{array}
\qquad
\begin{array}{r} 78 \\ + 7 \\ \hline \end{array}
\qquad
\begin{array}{r} 62 \\ + 17 \\ \hline \end{array}
\qquad
\begin{array}{r} 47 \\ + 16 \\ \hline \end{array}
\qquad
\begin{array}{r} 28 \\ + 37 \\ \hline \end{array}
$$

47

2.
$$
\begin{array}{r} 29 \\ + 23 \\ \hline \end{array}
\qquad
\begin{array}{r} 17 \\ + 27 \\ \hline \end{array}
\qquad
\begin{array}{r} 6 \\ + 76 \\ \hline \end{array}
\qquad
\begin{array}{r} 68 \\ + 8 \\ \hline \end{array}
\qquad
\begin{array}{r} 24 \\ + 27 \\ \hline \end{array}
\qquad
\begin{array}{r} 55 \\ + 4 \\ \hline \end{array}
$$

3.
$$
\begin{array}{r} 37 \\ + 25 \\ \hline \end{array}
\qquad
\begin{array}{r} 58 \\ + 4 \\ \hline \end{array}
\qquad
\begin{array}{r} 19 \\ + 36 \\ \hline \end{array}
\qquad
\begin{array}{r} 36 \\ + 35 \\ \hline \end{array}
\qquad
\begin{array}{r} 18 \\ + 66 \\ \hline \end{array}
\qquad
\begin{array}{r} 36 \\ + 57 \\ \hline \end{array}
$$

Problem Solving

Solve.

m a t h e m a _ _ _

4. Arturo made a word with his letters. He got 16 points for the word. He already had 39 points. What was his total score?

_____ points

Problem Solving

Use Data

Some children voted for their favorite
things to do in the summer. Count the tally marks.
Write the totals in the table.

Summer Activities		
	Tally Marks	Total
	ᚼᚼᚼ ᚼᚼᚼ ᚼᚼᚼ ᚼᚼᚼ ᚼᚼᚼ I	26
	ᚼᚼᚼ ᚼᚼᚼ ᚼᚼᚼ II	
	ᚼᚼᚼ III	
	ᚼᚼᚼ ᚼᚼᚼ III	

Answer the questions about the table.

1. How many children like
   to go camping in the
   summer?

   _____ children

2. What is the total number
   who like to skate and
   play baseball?

   _____ children

3. Which summer activity
   did the greatest number
   of children vote for?

   _____

   -

   _____

Story Corner

4. Make up a question
   about the table. Give it
   to a friend to answer.

Finding Reasonable Sums

Ring the best estimate.

1. Kenny has 39 cards.
   Kate has 24 cards.
   About how many
   cards do they have?

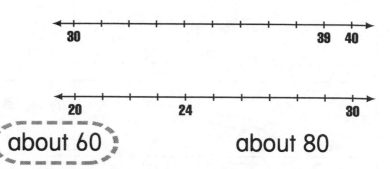

   about 40   (about 60)   about 80

2. Beth has 43 cards.
   Jack has 37 cards.
   About how many
   cards do they have?

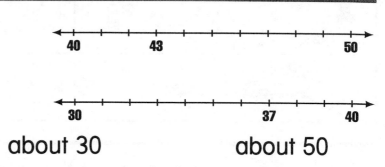

   about 80   about 30   about 50

3. Terry has 52 cards.
   Elena has 19 cards.
   About how many
   cards do they have?

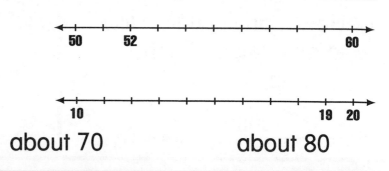

   about 60   about 70   about 80

Number Sense

Ring the best estimate.

4. $75 + 16$

   more than 70   more than 80   more than 90

Adding Money

Puzzle Sale

39¢   44¢   54¢   65¢

Use the picture.
Solve. Show your work.

1. Kim bought a
   clown puzzle
   and a boat
   puzzle. How
   much did
   she spend?

   $$\begin{array}{r} \overset{1}{54}¢ \\ +39¢ \\ \hline 93¢ \end{array}$$

   __93__ ¢

2. Ms. Tuma
   bought a boat
   puzzle and a
   tree puzzle.
   How much did
   she spend?

   _____ ¢
   _____ ¢
   _____ ¢

   _____ ¢

Ring the answer.

3. Carlos spent more than
   60¢ on one puzzle.   boat   tree   clown   jet
   Which puzzle did he buy?

Number Sense

Ring Yes or No.

4. Mark has 95¢. He wants   Yes   No
   to buy a jet puzzle and a
   boat puzzle. Does he
   have enough money?

Problem Solving

Too Little Information

Do you have enough information? If you do, solve.
If you do not, ring the sentence you need.
Then solve. Show your work.

1. In his first turn, Hank moved
   12 spaces on the game board.
   On his next turn, he moved
   11 spaces. How many spaces
   did he move?

   The board has 64 spaces.
   Hank has played the game
   8 times.

   _____ spaces

2. The game has two kinds of
   cards. It has 25 yellow cards.
   How many cards does the
   game have altogether?

   The game has 35 red cards.
   Hank played the game for
   20 minutes.

   _____ cards

Reasoning

Ring the answer.

3. A spinner has 4 numbers. The pattern
   of the numbers is + 2. What do you
   need to know to find the numbers?

   the sum of   any one of the   the first number
   the numbers   numbers

Exploring 2-Digit Subtraction

Complete the table.

	Show.	Take away.	Do you need to trade? Ring Yes or No.		Trade if you need to. Write how many are left.
1.	3 tens 4 ones	5 ones	(Yes)	No	_2_ tens _9_ ones
2.	4 tens 2 ones	7 ones	Yes	No	__ tens __ ones
3.	2 tens 2 ones	9 ones	Yes	No	__ tens __ ones
4.	3 tens 7 ones	6 ones	Yes	No	__ tens __ ones
5.	5 tens I one	8 ones	Yes	No	__ tens __ ones
6.	I ten 9 ones	9 ones	Yes	No	__ tens __ ones

Number Sense

7. Ring the better estimate.

$45 - 5 = 40$, so $45 - 8$ is   greater than 40

less than 40

73

Understanding 2-Digit Subtraction

Subtract. Trade if you need to.

1.
tens	ones
3	14
4̷	4̷
–	8
3	6

tens	ones
3	9
–	8

tens	ones
3	1
–	9

tens	ones
4	6
–	5

2.
tens	ones
3	3
–	4

tens	ones
2	4
–	7

tens	ones
2	5
–	8

tens	ones
4	8
–	9

3.
tens	ones
3	2
–	8

tens	ones
7	4
–	7

tens	ones
6	3
–	4

tens	ones
5	5
–	6

Number Sense

4. There are 59 windows. The man has washed 9. How many windows are left?

_____ windows

5. There are 23 houses. The woman has taken mail to 8. How many houses are left?

_____ houses

2-Digit Subtraction

Do you need to trade? Ring Yes or No.
Subtract.

1.

tens	ones	
5	8	Yes
−	3	(No)
5	5	

tens	ones	
4	3	Yes
−	2	No

tens	ones	
3	2	Yes
−	9	No

2.

tens	ones	
3	8	Yes
−	9	No

tens	ones	
3	5	Yes
−	7	No

tens	ones	
8	4	Yes
−	9	No

3.

tens	ones	
4	6	Yes
−	7	No

tens	ones	
3	2	Yes
−	9	No

tens	ones	
9	7	Yes
−	6	No

Number Sense

4. Tamara had 4 dimes and 7 pennies.
   She traded one of her dimes for 10
   pennies. Write how many dimes
   and pennies she has now. _____ dimes _____ pennies

More 2-Digit Subtraction

Do you need to trade?
Ring Yes or No.
Then subtract.

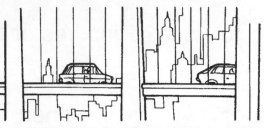

1.
$$\overset{5\ 15}{\cancel{6}5}$$ (Yes)   29 Yes   92 Yes   44 Yes
  −39   No   −17 No   −23 No   −21 No
   26

2.   54 Yes   74 Yes   99 Yes   81 Yes
   − 6 No   −57 No   −27 No   −24 No

3.   66 Yes   95 Yes   87 Yes   85 Yes
   −29 No   −16 No   − 6 No   −13 No

Problem Solving

Solve. Show your work.

4. Glen had 84¢. He paid
   25¢ to cross the
   bridge. How much
   did he have left?

   _____ ¢

5. Nicole had 5 dimes and
   7 pennies. She used 25¢
   to cross the bridge.
   What coins did
   she have left?   _____

   ____ dimes ____ pennies

More Subtraction

Subtract. Use the code to find
a secret message. Write the code
letter in the circle under each answer.

1.

29	92	44
−17	−23	−21
◯	◯	◯

54	66	56	94	60
−6	−40	−19	−15	−48
◯	◯	◯	◯	◯

88	77
−19	−15
◯	◯

91	59	97
−29	−28	−25
◯	◯	◯

79	42	85
−27	−5	−48
◯	◯	◯

CODE BOX

12	23	26	31	37	48	52	62	69	72	79
S	W	I	H	O	L	Z	T	A	E	N

Number Sense

2. Use the code. Make up a secret word.
   Write a subtraction sentence for each letter.
   Have a friend find your word.

Problem-Solving Strategy

Make and Use a Graph

A group of children collected jars.
Then they each made a graph.
They colored one jar on the graph
for each jar collected.
Here is Ken's graph.

Jars Collected

Week 1   🫙 🫙 🫙 🫙 🫙 🫙 🫙 🫙 🫙 🫙

Week 2   🫙 🫙 🫙 🫙 🫙 🫙 🫙 🫙 🫙 🫙

Week 3   🫙 🫙 🫙 🫙 🫙 🫙 🫙 🫙 🫙 🫙

Week 4   🫙 🫙 🫙 🫙 🫙 🫙 🫙 🫙 🫙 🫙

Color the jars.

1. Color 9 jars for Week 1.
2. Color 10 jars for Week 2.
3. Color 8 jars for Week 3.
4. Color 5 jars for Week 4.

Find the sum or difference.

5. How many jars did Ken collect
   in all for Weeks 2 and 3?

   _____ jars

6. How many more jars did Ken
   collect in Week 1 than in Week 4?

   _____ more jars

Visual Thinking

Do these without counting.

7. In which week did Ken
   collect the fewest jars?

   Week ___

8. In which week did Ken
   collect the most jars?

   Week ___

Checking Subtraction

Subtract. Then check by adding.

1.
$$\begin{array}{r} 67 \\ -12 \\ \hline 55 \end{array}$$
$$\begin{array}{r} 55 \\ +12 \\ \hline 67 \end{array}$$

$$\begin{array}{r} 87 \\ -48 \\ \hline \end{array}$$

$$\begin{array}{r} 92 \\ -57 \\ \hline \end{array}$$

2.
$$\begin{array}{r} 83 \\ -77 \\ \hline \end{array}$$

$$\begin{array}{r} 45 \\ -30 \\ \hline \end{array}$$

$$\begin{array}{r} 54 \\ -21 \\ \hline \end{array}$$

3.
$$\begin{array}{r} 61 \\ -32 \\ \hline \end{array}$$

$$\begin{array}{r} 80 \\ -28 \\ \hline \end{array}$$

$$\begin{array}{r} 72 \\ -55 \\ \hline \end{array}$$

Problem Solving

Solve. Show your work.

4. Suki drew 30 pictures last year. Bobby drew 19 pictures last year. How many more pictures did Suki draw?

_____ more pictures

5. Vince drew 27 pictures last year. He drew 15 pictures this year. How many pictures did he draw altogether?

_____ pictures

Adding and Subtracting Money

Add or subtract to solve.

1. Yolanda has 75¢. She buys one goldfish for 67¢. How much money does she have left?

$$
\begin{array}{r}
{}^{6}\cancel{7}{}^{15}\cancel{5}¢ \\
-67¢ \\
\hline
8¢
\end{array}
$$

____8____ ¢

2. Rita buys orange juice for 49¢ and grape juice for 67¢. How much more does the grape juice cost than the orange juice?

_____ ¢

3. Joel buys a pin for 32¢ and a ball for 56¢. How much money does he spend?

_____ ¢

4. Rob has 40¢. He wants to buy a boat that costs 88¢. How much more money does he need?

_____ ¢

Story Corner

Work with a friend.

5. Make up three word problems about buying things. Have your friend write a number sentence for each of your word problems.

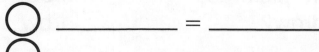
1. _____ ○ _____ = _____

2. _____ ○ _____ = _____

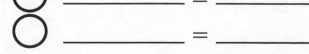
3. _____ ○ _____ = _____

Problem Solving

Choose the Operation

Add or subtract to solve.

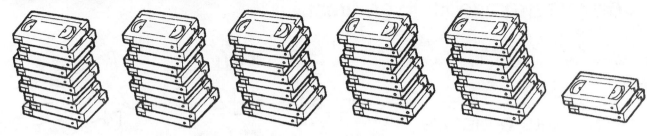

1. Albert counted 52 movie tapes. The store owner rented 36 of them. How many movie tapes were left?

_____16_____ movie tapes

2. Luisa counted 67 music tapes. Her friend Renée counted 14 more. How many music tapes did they count in all?

_____

_____ music tapes

3. Jeff has 37 tapes. Keith has 13 tapes. How many more tapes does Jeff have than Keith?

_____

_____ more tapes

Reasoning

Ring the best estimate.

4. Georgia used 11 tapes to fill a box. About how many tapes would she use to fill 4 boxes?

about 30
about 40
about 50

Addition and Subtraction Practice

Add or subtract. Find a pattern.
Connect the dots for the two sets of
answers, from least to greatest.

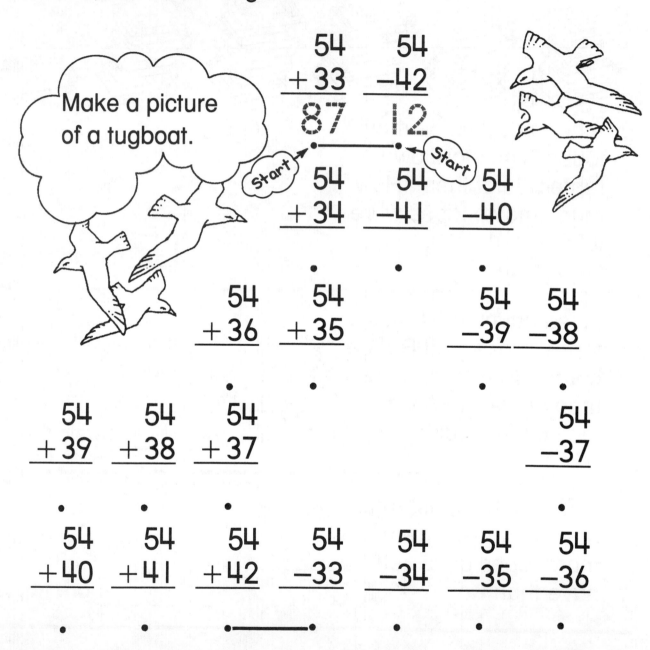

Make a picture of a tugboat.

$$
\begin{array}{r} 54 \\ +33 \\ \hline 87 \end{array}
\qquad
\begin{array}{r} 54 \\ -42 \\ \hline 12 \end{array}
$$

Start → •   • ← Start

$$
\begin{array}{r} 54 \\ +34 \\ \hline \end{array}
\qquad
\begin{array}{r} 54 \\ -41 \\ \hline \end{array}
\qquad
\begin{array}{r} 54 \\ -40 \\ \hline \end{array}
$$

$$
\begin{array}{r} 54 \\ +36 \\ \hline \end{array}
\qquad
\begin{array}{r} 54 \\ +35 \\ \hline \end{array}
\qquad
\begin{array}{r} 54 \\ -39 \\ \hline \end{array}
\qquad
\begin{array}{r} 54 \\ -38 \\ \hline \end{array}
$$

$$
\begin{array}{r} 54 \\ +39 \\ \hline \end{array}
\qquad
\begin{array}{r} 54 \\ +38 \\ \hline \end{array}
\qquad
\begin{array}{r} 54 \\ +37 \\ \hline \end{array}
\qquad
\begin{array}{r} 54 \\ -37 \\ \hline \end{array}
$$

$$
\begin{array}{r} 54 \\ +40 \\ \hline \end{array}
\quad
\begin{array}{r} 54 \\ +41 \\ \hline \end{array}
\quad
\begin{array}{r} 54 \\ +42 \\ \hline \end{array}
\quad
\begin{array}{r} 54 \\ -33 \\ \hline \end{array}
\quad
\begin{array}{r} 54 \\ -34 \\ \hline \end{array}
\quad
\begin{array}{r} 54 \\ -35 \\ \hline \end{array}
\quad
\begin{array}{r} 54 \\ -36 \\ \hline \end{array}
$$

Story Corner

Make up a word problem about
cars and trucks in a city. Have a
friend solve your problem.

82

Problem-Solving Strategy

Use Data

```
CESAR'S SPORTING GOODS
87 BASEBALLS      92 FOOTBALLS      36 SOCCER BALLS
79 BASKETBALLS    56 VOLLEYBALLS    43 GOLF BALLS
```

Use the poster to solve the problems.

1. How many more footballs are there than volleyballs?

   92
   −56
   ───
   36   _36_ more footballs

2. How many golf balls and soccer balls are there?

   ____

   _____ balls

3. How many volleyballs and golf balls are there?

   ____

   _____ balls

4. How many more basketballs are there than soccer balls?

   ____

   _____ more basketballs

5. 58 baseballs were sold. How many were not sold?

   ____

   _____ baseballs

6. 47 basketballs were sold. How many were not sold?

   ____

   _____ basketballs

Identifying Solid Shapes

1. Color each shape.

   ◯ green   ▭ yellow

   △ orange   ▱ purple

   ▯ red   △ blue

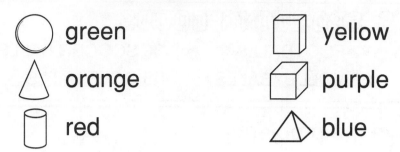

2. Count each shape.
   Write how many.

   __3__ ▱   _____ ▱

   _____ △   _____ ▯

   _____ ◯   _____ △

Visual Thinking

3. Tell a friend about one of the
   shapes on this page.
   Have your friend guess the shape.

Making Solid Shapes

Use cubes. Make the shape.
Tell how many cubes you used.

1.

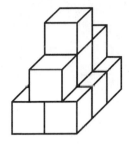

_____ cubes

2.

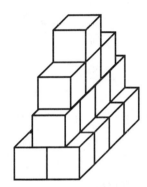

_____ cubes

Visual Thinking

3. Ring the shapes that have a round
bottom or a round top.

     cone   cube   cylinder

4. Ring the shapes that have corners.

     cube   rectangular prism   sphere

Making Plane Figures

1. Color inside the circles blue.
   Color inside the triangles orange.
   Color inside the rectangles red.

2. Count each shape. Write how many.

   _2_ circles   _____ triangles   _____ rectangles

3. Color inside the triangles purple.
   Color inside the circles red.
   Color inside the squares green.

4. How many are there? Count each shape.
   Write how many.

   _____ triangles   _____ circles   _____ squares

Visual Thinking

5. If you traced around the widest part
   of a cone, what plane figure would you draw?

   rectangle   circle   triangle

Sides and Corners

1. Draw a shape that has 8 sides and 8 corners.

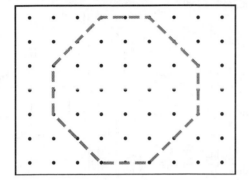

2. Draw a shape that has 5 sides and 5 corners.

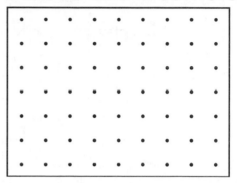

3. Draw a shape that has 3 sides and 3 corners.

4. Draw a shape that has 4 sides and 4 corners. All 4 sides are the same length.

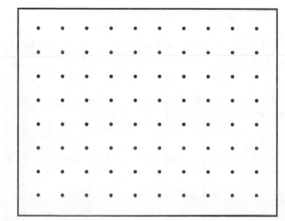

Visual Thinking

5. In this box, draw a shape that has sides and corners. Cover it.

   Describe it to a friend. Have your friend draw it. Compare your shape with the one your friend drew.

Extending a Pattern

Draw the shape that continues the pattern.

1.

_____

2.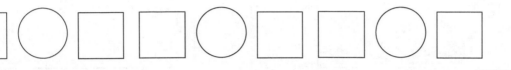

_____

3.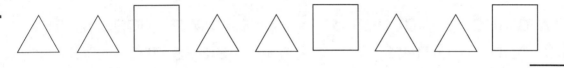

_____

4.

_____

5.

_____

6.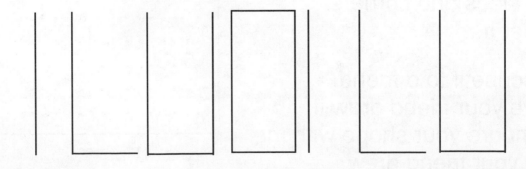

_____

Visual Thinking

Draw the shape that continues the pattern.

7.

_____

Congruent Figures

Look at each figure.
Use a geoboard to make a figure that is
the same size and shape.
Draw your figure.

1.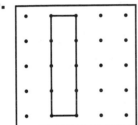

2.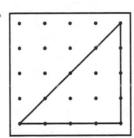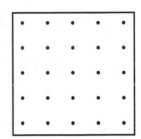

3.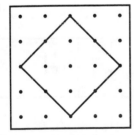

4.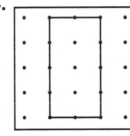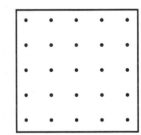

5.

6.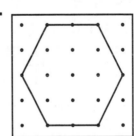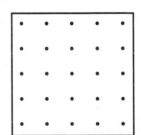

Reasoning

7. Use a pattern block. Copy this design.

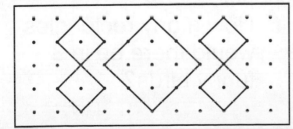 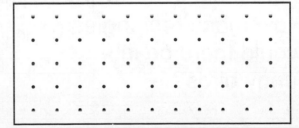

Problem-Solving Strategy

Make a Table

1. Some children made this funny bird.
    How many of each shape did they use?
    Complete the table to find out.

Our Funny Bird

Our Funny Bird	
Shape	Number
◯	2
▢	
▭	
△	

2. How many rectangles would there be in
    4 funny birds like this one?
    Make a table to find out.

birds	1	2	3	4
rectangles	5	——	——	——

Problem Solving

Use the table to answer the questions.

3. How many rectangles
    would there be in 4
    funny birds?

    _____

4. How many rectangles
    would there be in 3
    funny birds?

    _____

Symmetry

Draw one line of symmetry for each shape.

1.

2.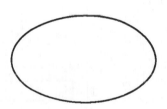

Draw two lines of symmetry for each shape.

3.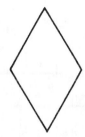

Visual Thinking

4. Ring the shape if it could be folded to make a line of symmetry.

  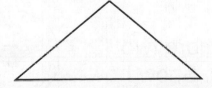 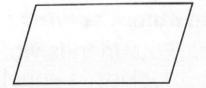

Equal Parts

Write the number of equal parts.

1.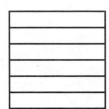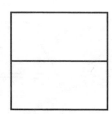

8
___   ___   ___   ___

2.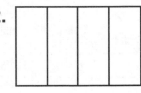

___   ___   ___   ___

3.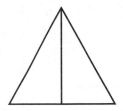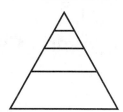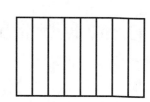

___   ___   ___   ___

4.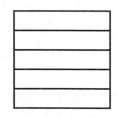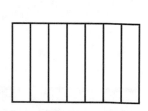

___   ___   ___   ___

Problem Solving

5. Four friends want to share two cookies in equal parts. Show how they can divide them.

Fractions

1. Color $\dfrac{1}{3}$.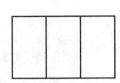

2. Color $\dfrac{1}{4}$.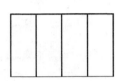

3. Color $\dfrac{1}{8}$.

Reasoning

Ring **Yes** or **No**.

4. Henry colored $\dfrac{1}{2}$ of a circle.

   Marsha colored $\dfrac{1}{2}$ of a larger circle.

   Did they color the same amount?

   Yes   No

More Fractions

Complete each fraction to show
what part is shaded.

1. 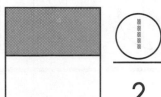 $\dfrac{1}{2}$  $\dfrac{}{3}$ $\dfrac{}{4}$

2. 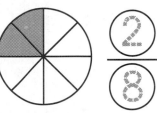 $\dfrac{}{8}$ 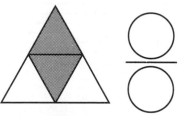 $\dfrac{}{6}$ 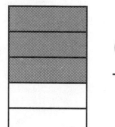 $\dfrac{}{5}$

Write a fraction to show what part is shaded.

3. 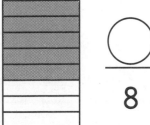 $\dfrac{2}{8}$ 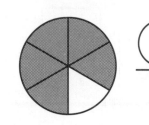 $\dfrac{}{}$ $\dfrac{}{}$

4. 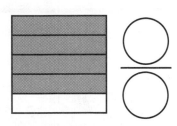 $\dfrac{}{}$ 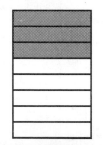 $\dfrac{}{}$ 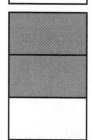 $\dfrac{}{}$

Visual Thinking

5. Ring the fractions that
are the same size.

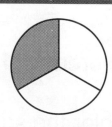 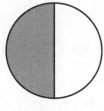 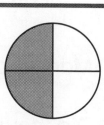

$\dfrac{1}{2}$ $\dfrac{1}{3}$ $\dfrac{2}{4}$

94

Parts of Groups

Color to show the fractions.

1.

$\frac{1}{3}$ green, $\frac{2}{3}$ yellow

2.

$\frac{2}{3}$ orange, $\frac{1}{3}$ red

3.

$\frac{2}{5}$ blue, $\frac{3}{5}$ orange

4.

$\frac{4}{5}$ purple, $\frac{1}{5}$ yellow

5.

$\frac{3}{4}$ green, $\frac{1}{4}$ purple

6.

$\frac{4}{6}$ red, $\frac{2}{6}$ blue

Problem Solving

Color. Write the answer.

How many trees are orange?

7. There are 4 trees.
   $\frac{1}{4}$ of the trees are yellow.
   The rest are orange.

_____ trees

95

Probability

Use a pencil and a paper clip
to make a spinner. Predict
which color the spinner
will stop on more often.
Ring the color.

black   gray

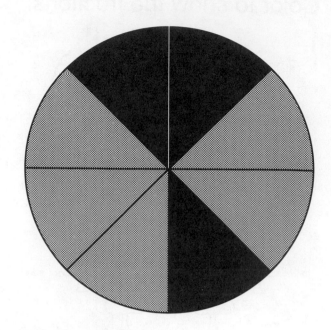

Spin the paper clip 10 times. Color the chart to
show where the spinner stops after each spin.

Spin	1	2	3	4	5	6	7	8	9	10
Black										
Gray										

Reasoning

Color the spinner so that it
will stop on black more often
than on gray. Try your
spinner.

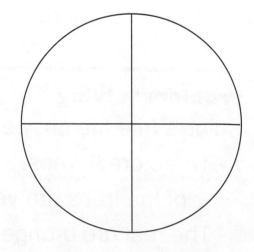

Problem-Solving Strategy

Draw a Picture

Some friends shared a cake.
Each decorated part of the cake.

Sara put raisins on her part.

Linda put nuts on her part.

Olga put coconut on her part.

Franco put lemon rings on his part.

Jack put blueberries on his part.

Kale put strawberries on his part.

1. Draw the cake so that each person gets an equal part.

Visual Thinking

Draw a picture to solve.
Ring the answer.

2. Sam and Elena shared a chicken pie. Sam ate $\frac{1}{4}$ of the pie. Elena ate $\frac{2}{4}$. How much pie was left?

$\frac{1}{4}$ $\frac{2}{4}$ $\frac{3}{4}$

Measuring Length

Use cubes to
measure each brush.
Write the length.

1.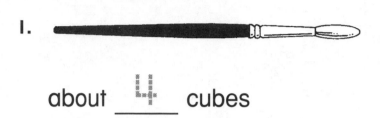

about ___4___ cubes

2.

about _____ cubes

3.

about _____ cubes

4.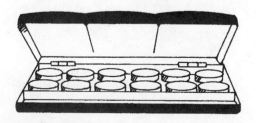

about _____ cubes

Visual Thinking

5. Ring the longer box.

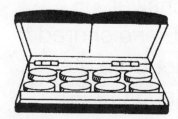

Inches and Feet

Use an inch ruler to draw pieces of yarn.

1. 2 inches

2. 5 inches

3. 3 inches

Ring in green the longest piece of yarn.
Ring in red the shortest piece of yarn.

Number Sense

Think about the real object.
Ring the better estimate.

4.

longer than I foot   longer than I foot

shorter than I foot   shorter than I foot

Problem-Solving Strategy
Estimate and Measure

Ring the reasonable answer.
Then use an inch ruler to measure the
length to the nearest inch.
Write the length.

		Estimate	Measure
1.	an eraser	1 inch (7 inches) 20 inches	about ____ inches
2.	your thumb	2 inches 9 inches 15 inches	about ____ inches
3.	a calculator	25 inches 15 inches 5 inches	about ____ inches

Number Sense

Write an estimate.

4.    about _____ long

Estimating and Measuring Weight

Nonstandard Units

Ring the one that weighs more.

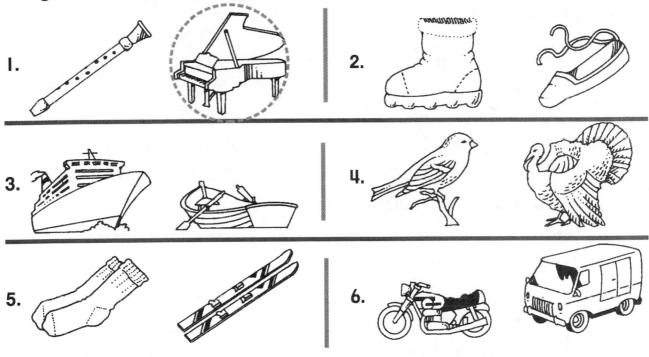

1.

2.

3.

4.

5.

6.

Ring the objects that weigh
less than you weigh.

7.

Story Corner

8. Work with a friend. Tell
   some things that weigh
   more than you weigh.

Estimating and Measuring Weight

Pounds

About how much does each weigh?
Ring the answer.

1.

about I pound
~~more than I pound~~
less than I pound

2.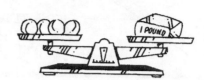

about I pound
more than I pound
less than I pound

3.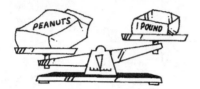

about one pound
more than I pound
less than I pound

4.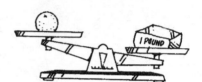

about one pound
more than I pound
less than I pound

Reasoning

Ring the correct picture.

5.

6.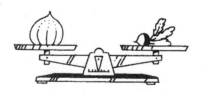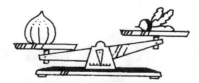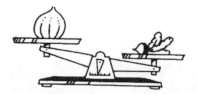

Quarts, Pints, and Cups

Which hold the same amounts?
Color the cups to show the amount.

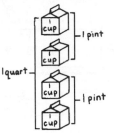

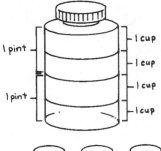

1. Pint

2. Quart

Solve.

3. Darren has 1 pint of juice. How many cups can he fill?

   __2__ cups

4. Marta has 1 quart of juice. How many cups can she fill?

   _____ cups

---

5. Lani has 3 cups of juice. Beth has 1 quart of juice. Who has more juice?

   _____

   _____

6. Kim has 1 quart of juice. He drinks 1 cup of it. How much does he have left?

   _____

   _____

Number Sense

Ring the better estimate.

7.

   more than 1 quart
   less than 1 quart

8.

   more than 1 cup
   less than 1 cup

Choose the Appropriate Tool

Ring the right tool for the job.

1. To find the length of a board

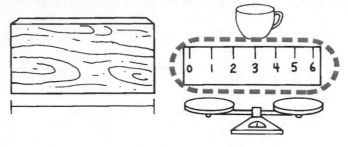

2. To find the amount of juice in a bottle

3. To find out whether a rock weighs more than a shell

 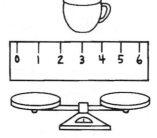

4. To find the length of a nail

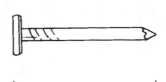 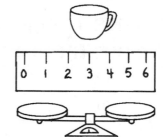

Story Corner

5. Work with a friend. Pretend you are making a bird feeder. Tell what tools you would use to measure.

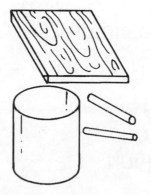 

Centimeters

Use your centimeter ruler to draw pieces
of yarn.

1. 7 centimeters

2. 3 centimeters

3. 11 centimeters

This string is 10 centimeters
long. It is 1 decimeter long.
Work with a friend.
4. Measure and cut a string that
   is as long as a decimeter.
   Use your string to find
   something that is longer.
   Write the name of the
   object you found.

_____

- - - - - - - - - - - - - - -

_____

Number Sense

5. Hal's card is 3 centimeters wider than
   Meg's. Meg's card is 7 centimeters
   wide. How wide is Hal's card?   _____ centimeters

Perimeter

Use your centimeter ruler to measure the perimeter.

1.

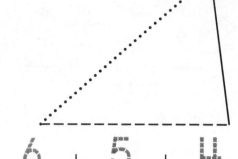

$$\underline{6} + \underline{5} + \underline{4} = \underline{15}$$ centimeters

The perimeter of the triangle is $\underline{15}$ centimeters.

2.

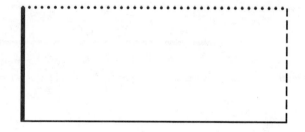

$$\underline{} + \underline{} + \underline{} + \underline{} = \underline{}$$ centimeters

3.

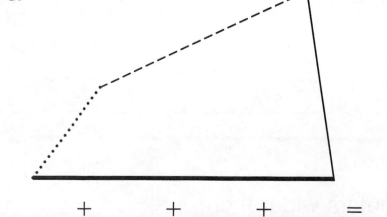

$$\underline{} + \underline{} + \underline{} + \underline{} = \underline{}$$ centimeters

Kilograms

Read each scale. Then write the weight.

1.

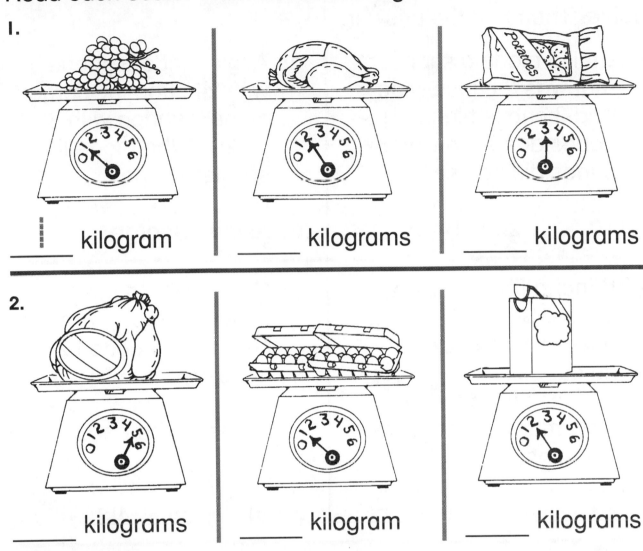

_____ kilogram

_____ kilograms

_____ kilograms

2.

_____ kilograms

_____ kilogram

_____ kilograms

Reasoning

Ring the better estimate.

3. About how much does a brick weigh?

    2 kilograms   20 kilograms

4. About how much does a book weigh?

    1 kilogram   10 kilograms

Volume

Use cubes and a box.
Solve. Then ring the answer.

1. Emilio made a shape that was 2 cubes wide and 2 cubes high and 3 cubes deep. How many cubes did he use?

   10   (12)   14

2. Angie made a shape with 24 cubes. George made a shape with 32 cubes. Who made the smaller shape?

   Angie   George

3. Winona filled a box with cubes. She covered the bottom of the box with 20 cubes. Three layers of cubes filled the box. How many cubes were in the box?

   40   50   60

4. Greg covered the bottom of a box with 12 cubes. He needed 2 more layers to fill the box. How many more cubes did he need?

   24   36   48

Visual Thinking

5. Ring the cubes that are easier to count.

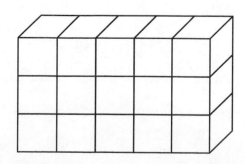
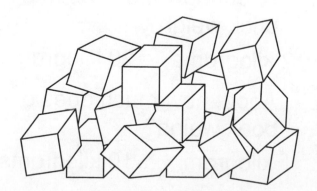

Temperature

Fahrenheit and Celsius

Use a Fahrenheit thermometer and a red crayon.

1. Look at the thermometer. Color to show the temperature.

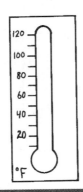

2. Put the thermometer in a glass of hot water. Wait 5 minutes. Read the temperature. Color to show the temperature.

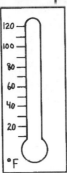

Use a Celsius thermometer and a red crayon.

3. Look at the thermometer. Color to show the temperature.

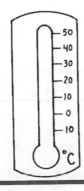

4. Put the thermometer on an ice cube. Wait 5 minutes. Read the temperature. Color to show the temperature.

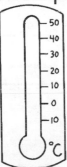

Number Sense

Ring the better estimate.

5. 30 degrees Fahrenheit
   90 degrees Fahrenheit

Problem-Solving Strategy

Guess and Check

How many 1-inch punch-out squares will
fit in each space?
First, write your guess.
Then use 1-inch squares to check.

1.

Guess. _____ squares   Check. __10__ squares

2.

Guess. _____ squares   Check. _____ squares

3.

Guess. _____ squares

Check. _____ squares

Exploring Hundreds

Use hundreds to show each number.
Write the number.

1.  2 hundred _200_

2. 4 hundred ____

3. 6 hundred ____

4. 8 hundred ____

5. 9 hundred ____

6. 7 hundred ____

7. 5 hundred ____

8. 3 hundred ____

9. 1 hundred ____

Number Sense

Write the numbers.

10. ____

11. ____

111

Exploring 3-Digit Numbers

Count. Write the number.

1. ___3___ hundreds ___2___ tens ___4___ ones **324**

2. _____ hundreds _____ tens _____ one _____

3. _____ hundreds _____ tens _____ ones _____

Reasoning

Ring the most reasonable answer.

4. Cliff is _____ years older than his brother.

   8   80   800

5. There are _____ children in the full school bus.

   4   40   400

6. There are _____ seats in the movie house.

   2   20   200

7. The movie is _____ hours long.

   3   30   300

Understanding Hundreds, Tens, and Ones

Work with a friend.
Use place-value models.

1. Show the number. Add 10 more. Continue adding 10 more. Complete the table.

	hundreds	tens	ones
640	6	4	0
650	6	5	0

2. Show the number. Add 100 more. Continue adding 100 more. Complete the table.

	hundreds	tens	ones
300	3	0	0

Number Sense

Ring the models that show the same number.
Use place-value models if you need to.

3.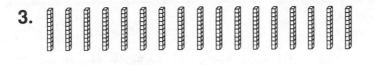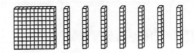

Writing Numbers to 999

Look at the models.
Write how many in the chart.
Then write the number.

1.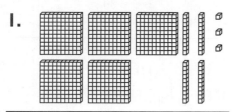

hundreds	tens	ones
5	4	3

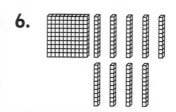 543

2.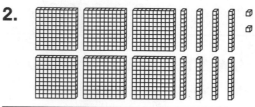

hundreds	tens	ones

_____

3.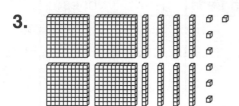

hundreds	tens	ones

_____

4.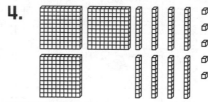

hundreds	tens	ones

_____

5.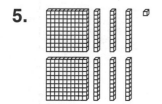

hundreds	tens	ones

_____

6.

hundreds	tens	ones

_____

Number Sense

7. Write the number that is 10 greater than 173.

_____

8. Write the number that is 100 greater than 731.

_____

114

Place Value

Read the number in the chart. Write how many.

1.

hundreds	tens	ones
7	2	8

___7___ hundreds 700

___2___ tens 20

___8___ ones 8

hundreds	tens	ones
2	7	8

_____ hundreds _____

_____ tens _____

_____ ones _____

2.

hundreds	tens	ones
5	1	6

_____ hundreds _____

_____ tens _____

_____ ones _____

hundreds	tens	ones
6	5	1

_____ hundreds _____

_____ tens _____

_____ ones _____

3.

hundreds	tens	ones
4	3	7

_____ hundreds _____

_____ tens _____

_____ ones _____

hundreds	tens	ones
3	4	7

_____ hundreds _____

_____ tens _____

_____ ones _____

Number Sense

4. Lucas has 7 ones and 9 hundreds. What number is he showing?

_____

5. Vicki has 2 tens and 6 hundreds. What number is she showing?

_____

115

More Place Value

Write the number.

1. 4 hundreds 8 tens 7 ones   487

2. 500 + 50 + 2   _____

3. 800 + 7   _____

4. 6 hundreds 1 ten 1 one   _____

Work with a friend.

5. Fill in the puzzle.

Across

1. 199 + 1
2. 400 + 50
4. 3, 6, _____, 12
5. 7 hundreds 1 ten 8 ones
6. 400 + 50 + 6
9. 700 + 80 + 9
11. 5 hundreds 7 tens 3 ones
13. 200 + 300
14. 4, 8, 12, _____
15. 1 more than 997

Down

1. 2 hundreds 9 tens 4 ones
2. 4 hundreds 1 ten 7 ones
3. 500 + 80 + 8
7. 500 + 50 + 5
8. 6 hundreds 7 tens
10. 900 + 6
12. 1 more than 308
14. 9, _____, 27, 36

Number Sense

6. Write the number that is 3 hundreds less than 640. _____

Problem-Solving Strategy

Make a Bar Graph

What is the favorite forest animal of your friends?
Ask each child to choose his or her favorite animal.
Write a tally mark / to show each answer.
Find the total for each animal.
Then complete your graph.

1.

Animal	Tally Marks	Total
Rabbit		
Squirrel		
Deer		
Raccoon		

2.

Favorite Animal

Rabbit															
Squirrel															
Deer															
Raccoon															

0　1　2　3　4　5　6　7　8　9　10　11　12　13　14　15

Visual Thinking

3. Which bar on your graph shows
you the least favorite animal?

Ring it.　　　longest bar　　　shortest bar

After, Before, Between

Count.
Write the number that comes after.

1. 333, 334   549, _____   385, _____

2. 241, _____   709, _____   400, _____

Count.
Write the number that comes before.

3. _____, 694   _____, 377   _____, 249

4. _____, 599   _____, 320   _____, 201

Count.
Write the number that comes between.

5. 562, _____, 564   375, _____, 377   872, _____, 874

6. 363, _____, 365   542, _____, 544   299, _____, 301

Visual Thinking

Draw the missing shapes.
7. heart, diamond, heart, diamond, heart, _____, _____, diamond, heart

8. diamond, diamond, heart, diamond, diamond, heart, _____, _____, heart, diamond, diamond

Comparing Numbers

Write each number.
Compare. Then ring the number that is less.

1.

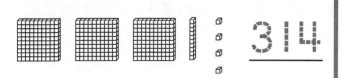 314

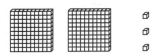 _____

2.

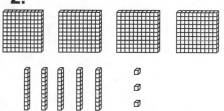 _____

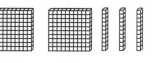 _____

3.

 _____

_____

4.

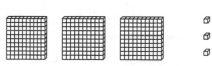 _____

_____

Number Sense

Use place-value models to compare.
Then ring the number that is less.

5.				
167	578	823	424	169
176	478	923	323	109

More Comparing Numbers

Write < or > in the ◯.

1. 139 ◯ 193   390 ◯ 391   421 ◯ 422

2. 598 ◯ 498   401 ◯ 441   509 ◯ 501

3. 777 ◯ 771   902 ◯ 992   120 ◯ 102

4. 99 ◯ 100   999 ◯ 99   287 ◯ 267

5. 302 ◯ 320   675 ◯ 576   110 ◯ 101

Number Sense

Write the numbers in order from least to greatest.
Use place-value models if you need to.

6. 13, 621, 27, 98, 109, 56, 129

13, _____, _____, _____, _____, _____, 621

82, 208, 802, 28, 280, 820

28, _____, _____, _____, _____, _____

Counting Patterns

Use your calculator. Write each number you see.

1. Press

ON/C 2 0 + = = = = =

$\underline{20}$ $\underline{40}$ ___ ___ ___ ___

2. Press

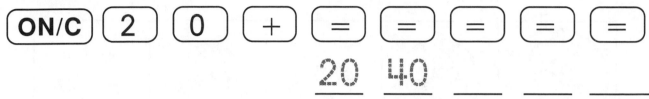

ON/C 5 7 + 1 0 = = =

___ ___ ___

3. Press

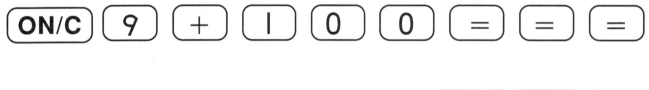

ON/C 9 + 1 0 0 = = =

___ ___ ___

Reasoning

Write each number.

4. I am 50 less than 300.
   I am 10 more than 240.
   What number am I?

   ___

5. I am 100 more than 830.
   I am 50 less than 980.
   What number am I?

   ___

Dollar

Work with a friend.
Take turns showing ways to make $1.00.
Write how many.

1. 1	1	0	0	25
2.				
3.				
4.				
5.				

Number Sense

6. Ring the coins that show the same
amount of money.

122

Dollar and Cents

Ring how much money is needed.
Use punch-out money to help you.

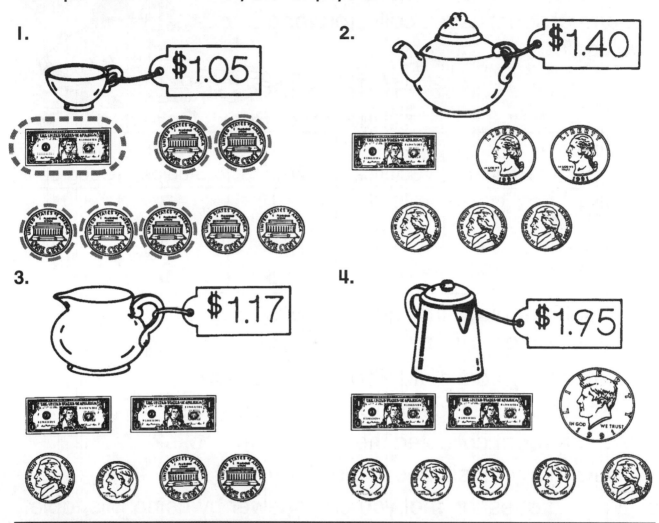

1. $1.05

2. $1.40

3. $1.17

4. $1.95

Problem Solving

5. Nick has 1 dollar and 3 nickels. Lola has 5 quarters. Write how much each child has. Then ring the greater amount.

Nick has _____

Lola has _____

6. Debra has [image]. She wants to buy [image] $1.30. Does she have enough money?
Ring **Yes** or **No**.

Yes

No

Problem Solving

Write Appropriate Questions

This table shows how many books the second-grade classes collected for a book sale.

Number of Books Collected

Room Number	Reading	Science	Math	Social Studies	Geography
130	19	17	11	7	4
131	18	15	18	13	5
132	9	10	13	8	14

Look at the table. Ring the questions that you can answer by using the table.

1. How many books did Room 133 collect?

   How many science books were collected?

2. Which room collected the most math books?

   How many music books did Room 132 collect?

3. Write a question that you can answer by using this table.

_____

- -

_____

_____

- -

_____

Story Corner

4. Make up other questions about this table. Tell them to a friend.
   Have your friend answer each question.

Adding Hundreds

Look for a pattern.
Add in your head. Then write the sums.

1.
$$\begin{array}{r} 2 \\ +2 \\ \hline 4 \end{array}$$ $$\begin{array}{r} 2 \\ +3 \\ \hline \end{array}$$ $$\begin{array}{r} 2 \\ +4 \\ \hline \end{array}$$ $$\begin{array}{r} 2 \\ +5 \\ \hline \end{array}$$ $$\begin{array}{r} 2 \\ +6 \\ \hline \end{array}$$ $$\begin{array}{r} 2 \\ +7 \\ \hline \end{array}$$

2.
$$\begin{array}{r} 20 \\ +20 \\ \hline \end{array}$$ $$\begin{array}{r} 20 \\ +30 \\ \hline \end{array}$$ $$\begin{array}{r} 20 \\ +40 \\ \hline \end{array}$$ $$\begin{array}{r} 20 \\ +50 \\ \hline \end{array}$$ $$\begin{array}{r} 20 \\ +60 \\ \hline \end{array}$$ $$\begin{array}{r} 20 \\ +70 \\ \hline \end{array}$$

3.
$$\begin{array}{r} 200 \\ +200 \\ \hline \end{array}$$ $$\begin{array}{r} 200 \\ +300 \\ \hline \end{array}$$ $$\begin{array}{r} 200 \\ +400 \\ \hline \end{array}$$ $$\begin{array}{r} 200 \\ +500 \\ \hline \end{array}$$ $$\begin{array}{r} 200 \\ +600 \\ \hline \end{array}$$ $$\begin{array}{r} 200 \\ +700 \\ \hline \end{array}$$

4.
$$\begin{array}{r} 100 \\ +800 \\ \hline \end{array}$$ $$\begin{array}{r} 100 \\ +700 \\ \hline \end{array}$$ $$\begin{array}{r} 100 \\ +600 \\ \hline \end{array}$$ $$\begin{array}{r} 100 \\ +500 \\ \hline \end{array}$$ $$\begin{array}{r} 100 \\ +400 \\ \hline \end{array}$$ $$\begin{array}{r} 100 \\ +300 \\ \hline \end{array}$$

Visual Thinking

5. Match each problem to the model that shows the sum.

$$\begin{array}{r} 9 \\ +5 \\ \hline \end{array}$$

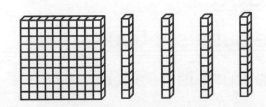

$$\begin{array}{r} 90 \\ +50 \\ \hline \end{array}$$

Exploring 3-Digit Addition

Use place-value models.
Find the sums. Trade if you need to.

1.

hundreds	tens	ones
	⬚1	
3	6	8
+ 1	1	3
4	8	1

hundreds	tens	ones
	☐	
1	8	7
+ 2	1	2

hundreds	tens	ones
	☐	
7	3	4
+	3	6

2.

hundreds	tens	ones
	☐	
4	1	3
+ 3	1	9

hundreds	tens	ones
	☐	
5	5	5
+	4	3

hundreds	tens	ones
	☐	
6	2	7
+ 2	4	6

Number Sense

Ring your estimate.

> Remember
> < means less than
> > means greater than

3. 400
     + 300

The sum is < 500.

The sum is > 500.

4. 100
     + 700

The sum is < 900.

The sum is > 900.

Understanding 3-Digit Addition

Use place-value models. Add.

1.

hundreds	tens	ones
2	3	7
+ 5	0	2
7	3	9

hundreds	tens	ones
4	2	9
+ 1	1	6

hundreds	tens	ones
3	3	8
+ 2	2	6

2.

hundreds	tens	ones
2	2	5
+ 1	6	6

hundreds	tens	ones
3	6	8
+ 1	1	1

hundreds	tens	ones
2	0	3
+ 2	5	8

3.

hundreds	tens	ones
7	3	9
+ 1	4	2

hundreds	tens	ones
3	6	7
+	1	3

hundreds	tens	ones
5	2	3
+ 1	0	6

Problem Solving

Solve.

4. There are 329 cans of peanuts. There are 221 cans of walnuts. How many cans of nuts are there in all?

_____ cans

5. Rick counted 102 boxes of oat cereal. He counted 89 boxes of corn cereal. How many boxes of cereal did he count in all?

_____ boxes

Adding 3-Digit Numbers

Use place-value models. Add.

1.

hundreds	tens	ones
2	7	3
+ 1	6	4
4	3	7

hundreds	tens	ones
5	6	1
+	1	9

hundreds	tens	ones
2	7	8
+ 2	1	1

2.

hundreds	tens	ones
3	5	4
+ 3	0	6

hundreds	tens	ones
6	7	0
+ 2	4	9

hundreds	tens	ones
4	0	5
+ 5	2	8

3.

$$834 \quad 242 \quad 468 \quad 106 \quad 333 \quad 691$$
$$+\ 82 \quad +666 \quad +426 \quad +\ 516 \quad +465 \quad +\ 118$$

Problem Solving

Solve. Use a calculator.

4. Ian clipped the wool of 348 sheep. Nell clipped 292 sheep. How many sheep did they clip in all?

_____ sheep

5. There are 168 hours in one week. How many hours are in 2 weeks?

_____ hours

More Adding 3-Digit Numbers

Add.

1.
$$\begin{array}{r} 629 \\ +154 \\ \hline 783 \end{array}$$
$$\begin{array}{r} 439 \\ +258 \\ \hline \end{array}$$
$$\begin{array}{r} 432 \\ +483 \\ \hline \end{array}$$
$$\begin{array}{r} 562 \\ +396 \\ \hline \end{array}$$
$$\begin{array}{r} 135 \\ +593 \\ \hline \end{array}$$

2.
$$\begin{array}{r} 537 \\ +\ 23 \\ \hline \end{array}$$
$$\begin{array}{r} 516 \\ +133 \\ \hline \end{array}$$
$$\begin{array}{r} 608 \\ +347 \\ \hline \end{array}$$
$$\begin{array}{r} 320 \\ +497 \\ \hline \end{array}$$
$$\begin{array}{r} 256 \\ +316 \\ \hline \end{array}$$

3.
$$\begin{array}{r} 725 \\ +154 \\ \hline \end{array}$$
$$\begin{array}{r} 154 \\ +\ 29 \\ \hline \end{array}$$
$$\begin{array}{r} 390 \\ +595 \\ \hline \end{array}$$
$$\begin{array}{r} 456 \\ +293 \\ \hline \end{array}$$
$$\begin{array}{r} 708 \\ +\ 58 \\ \hline \end{array}$$

Problem Solving

Solve.

4. The supermarket has 134 cans of vegetables and 290 cans of fruit. How many cans are there in all?

_____ cans

5. There are 236 bottles of apple juice and 328 bottles of grape juice. How many bottles are there in all?

_____ bottles

Problem Solving

Use a Graph

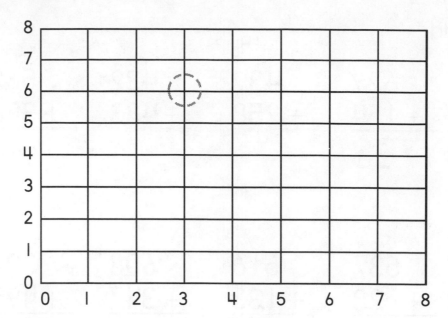

Follow these directions.
Draw a ring at the crossing point.

1. Start at 0. Go → 3. Go ↑ 6.
   Draw an orange ring at the crossing point.

2. Start at 0. Go → 1. Go ↑ 3.
   Draw a black ring at the crossing point.

3. Start at 0. Go → 5. Go ↑ 5.
   Draw a red ring at the crossing point.

4. Start at 0. Go → 7. Go ↑ 4.
   Draw a green ring at the crossing point.

Reasoning

5. Start at 0. Go → 6. Go ← 6.
   Where are you? Ring the answer.

   0   3   6

Subtracting Hundreds

Look for a pattern.
Subtract in your head. Then write the difference.

1.
$$7 - 6 \qquad 7 - 5 \qquad 7 - 4 \qquad 7 - 3 \qquad 7 - 2 \qquad 7 - 1$$

2.
$$70 - 60 \qquad 70 - 50 \qquad 70 - 40 \qquad 70 - 30 \qquad 70 - 20 \qquad 70 - 10$$

3.
$$700 - 600 \qquad 700 - 500 \qquad 700 - 400 \qquad 700 - 300 \qquad 700 - 200 \qquad 700 - 100$$

Solve. Use a  .

4. $400 + 400 - 300 - 100 = $ _____

5. $300 - 200 + 600 + 200 = $ _____

Visual Thinking

6. Match each problem to the model that shows the difference.

$$12 - 8$$

$$120 - 80$$

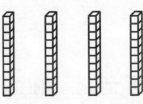

Exploring 3-Digit Subtraction

Use place-value models.
Find the difference. Trade if you need to.

1.

hundreds	tens	ones
	7	11
2	8	1
− 1	6	4
1	1	7

hundreds	tens	ones
	□	□
6	7	3
− 4	4	9

hundreds	tens	ones
	□	□
8	8	7
− 3	2	8

2.

hundreds	tens	ones
	□	□
4	5	6
− 1	2	8

hundreds	tens	ones
	□	□
4	9	0
− 1	7	2

hundreds	tens	ones
	□	□
6	5	4
− 3	3	8

3.

hundreds	tens	ones
	□	□
4	2	1
− 2	1	6

hundreds	tens	ones
□	□	
3	4	2
−	2	4

hundreds	tens	ones
	□	□
5	8	1
− 1	5	9

Number Sense

Ring the better estimate.

4.
```
  500
− 100
```

The difference is < 300.

The difference is > 300.

5.
```
  500
− 300
```

The difference is < 300.

The difference is > 300.

Understanding 3-Digit Subtraction

Use place-value models.
Find the differences. Trade if you need to.

1.

hundreds	tens	ones
	5	18
7	6	8
− 3	2	9
4	3	9

hundreds	tens	ones
8	5	3
− 4	0	5

hundreds	tens	ones
6	8	2
−	1	7

2.

hundreds	tens	ones
6	3	5
− 1	0	7

hundreds	tens	ones
7	5	4
− 6	2	5

hundreds	tens	ones
8	2	3
− 5	1	2

3.

$$576 - 69 \qquad 472 - 256 \qquad 683 - 244 \qquad 756 - 135 \qquad 470 - 244$$

Problem Solving

4. There are 352 monkeys and 218 lions in the park. How many more monkeys are there than lions?

_____ more monkeys

5. There are 250 hippos in the park. 32 hippos are babies. The rest are adults. How many adults hippos are there?

_____ adult hippos

Subtracting 3-Digit Numbers

Use place-value models. Subtract.

1.

hundreds	tens	ones
4	1	9
− 2	2	5
1	9	4

hundreds	tens	ones
5	7	6
− 1	8	3

hundreds	tens	ones
2	3	5
−	1	8

2.

hundreds	tens	ones
8	2	1
− 5	0	1

hundreds	tens	ones
6	4	2
− 2	7	1

hundreds	tens	ones
7	3	3
− 3	4	3

3.

$$958 - 42 \qquad 600 - 200 \qquad 313 - 182 \qquad 504 - 372 \qquad 972 - 656$$

Problem Solving

Solve.

4. Use your calculator. Subtract. Then read the answer upside down. Write the word.

   864
   − 519   _____

5. The teacher has 442 math books and 327 science books. How many more math books than science books does he have?

   _____ more math books

Estimating Sums and Differences

About how much does each bunch of
flowers cost?
Write the amount.

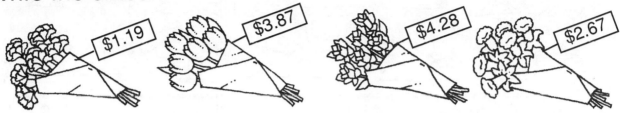

1.

$1.00 _____ _____ _____

First, estimate the total cost.
Then use a calculator to find the total cost.

2.

 $1.19    $3.87    $4.28

 $3.87   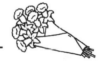 $2.67 $1.19

Estimate: $5.00   Estimate: _____   Estimate: _____

Answer: $5.06   Answer: _____   Answer: _____

Number Sense

3. About how much is left? Ring the better estimate.
Use a calculator to find the answer.

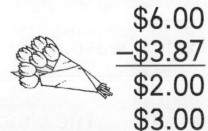
$3.00
−$1.19
$2.00
$3.00

$6.00
−$3.87
$2.00
$3.00

$5.00
−$4.28
$2.00
$1.00

Problem Solving

Identify Reasonable Results

Bagel with Cheese	$1.49	2 Pickles	$1.10
I pound of Potato Salad	$2.85	Hero Sandwich	$4.40
Tuna Fish Sandwich	$3.75		

Estimate to find if the total cost is reasonable.
Then ring **Yes** or **No**.

1. Renée buys a bagel with cheese and 2 pickles. The total cost is about $1.00.

$$\begin{array}{r} \$1.00 \\ +\ \$1.00 \\ \hline \$2.00 \end{array}$$

Yes (No)

2. Pablo buys I tuna fish sandwich and I pound of potato salad. The total cost is about $5.00.

Yes   No

_____

3. Adrienne buys I hero sandwich and 2 pickles. The total cost is about $5.00.

Yes   No

_____

Reasoning

4. Ring the better estimate.
   Evan buys a bagel with cheese.
   He pays $2.00.

   The change is < $1.00.   The change is > $1.00.

Making Equal Groups

Work with a friend.
Use cubes to show equal groups.
Then draw equal groups of dots on the clown hats.

1. 2 groups of 4

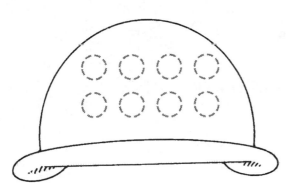

2. 3 groups of 4

3. 3 groups of 2

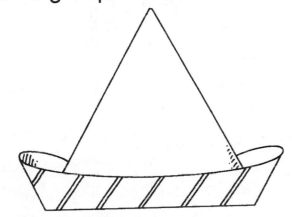

4. 4 groups of 5

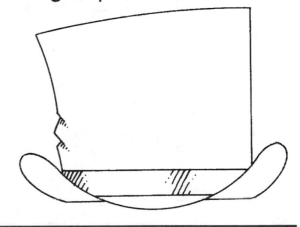

Number Sense

5. Ring the picture that shows equal groups.

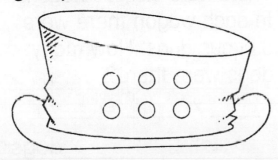

Exploring Multiplication with 2 and 5

Ring groups of 2 shoes. Complete the
sentences to find out how many shoes there are.

1.

2 + 2 + 2 = __6__

3 equal groups of 2 = __6__

__3__ x 2 = __6__

2.

2 + 2 + 2 + 2 = _____

4 equal groups of 2 = _____

_____ x 2 = _____

3.

2 + 2 = _____

2 equal groups of 2 = _____

_____ x 2 = _____

4.

2 + 2 + 2 + 2 + 2 = _____

5 equal groups of 2 = _____

_____ x 2 = _____

Problem Solving

Use cubes. Write a number sentence to solve.

5. There were 5 jugglers in
the circus. Each juggler
had 5 balls. How many
balls were there?

_____ x _____ = _____

_____ balls

6. There were 5 circus wagons.
In each wagon there were
3 circus dogs. How many
dogs were there?

_____ x _____ = _____

_____ dogs

Multiplying with 3 and 4

Use punch-out dollars.
Complete the multiplication sentences.

1.

Ring groups of 3.

__2__ x $3 = $__6__

2.

Ring groups of 3.

_____ x $3 = $_____

3.

Ring groups of 4.

_____ x $4 = $_____

4.

Ring groups of 4.

_____ x $4 = $_____

Visual Thinking

Ring the answer.

5. Which stacks would be higher,
   4 stacks of 5 umbrellas, or
   5 stacks of 4 umbrellas?

4 stacks of 5 umbrellas

5 stacks of 4 umbrellas

Vertical Multiplication

Use cubes. Write the multiplication fact both ways.

1.

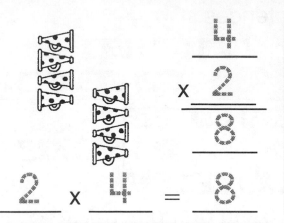

$$\begin{array}{r} 4 \\ \times\ 2 \\ \hline 8 \end{array}$$

_2_ x _4_ = _8_

2.

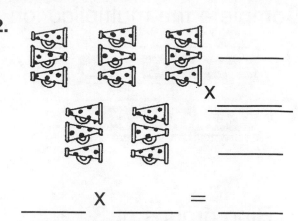

_____ x _____ = _____

3.

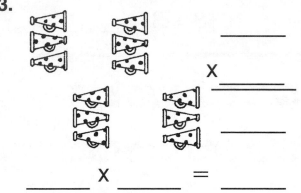

_____ x _____ = _____

4.

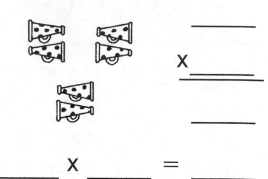

_____ x _____ = _____

5.

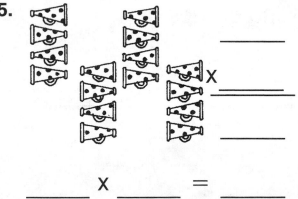

_____ x _____ = _____

6.

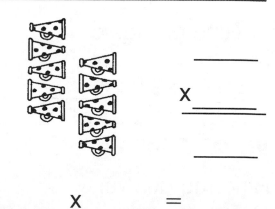

_____ x _____ = _____

Story Corner

7. Make up a clown story about any multiplication fact. Tell your story to a friend. Write the fact two ways.

140

Understanding Multiplication

Use cubes. Write each product.

1.

   1 x 3 = _3_

2.

   4 x 1 = ____

3.

   4 x 5 = ____

4.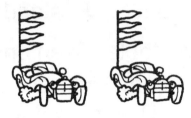

   2 x 4 = ____

Use cubes. Multiply.

5.
$$\begin{array}{ccccc} 2 & 1 & 4 & 1 & 3 \\ \underline{\times\ 1} & \underline{\times\ 5} & \underline{\times\ 1} & \underline{\times\ 1} & \underline{\times\ 1} \end{array}$$

Reasoning

Use cubes. Ring the answer.

6. Put 1 group of 0 cubes on your mat. Put 2 groups of 0 cubes on your mat. How many cubes are on your mat?

   2 cubes   1 cube   0 cubes

7. You have 4 baskets. There are 0 apples in each basket. How many apples do you have in all?

   0 apples   2 apples   4 apples

Problem Solving

Use a Graph

Children Who Went to the Circus

Group A	🚶 🚶 🚶 🚶 🚶
Group B	🚶 🚶 🚶 🚶
Group C	🚶 🚶
Group D	🚶 🚶 🚶

Each 🚶 stands for 4 children.

Read the table. Then answer each question.

1. How many children in Group D went to the circus?

   __12__ children

2. How many children in Group B went to the circus?

   _____ children

3. Which group has the fewest children who went to the circus?

   Group _____

4. What is the total number of children in Groups A and C who went to the circus?

   _____ children

Reasoning

Suppose each 🚶 meant 2 children. Ring the answers.

5. Would your answer to question 3 change?

      Yes   No

6. What would your answer to question 2 be now?

   8 children   32 children

Multiplication in Any Order

Use punch-out hankies.
Write the number sentence.

1.

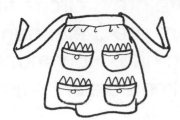

__4__ x __5__ = __20__

2.

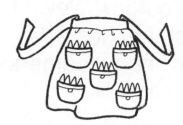

__5__ x __4__ = __20__

3.

_____ x _____ = _____

4.

_____ x _____ = _____

5.

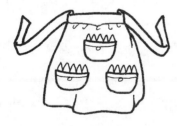

_____ x _____ = _____

6.

_____ x _____ = _____

Story Corner

7. Work with a friend.
Tell a story about the picture.
Then write a number sentence.

_____

- -

_____

Multiplying with a Calculator

Use a calculator for skip-counting and multiplying.

1. Alicia has 4 clown hats. Each hat has 3 feathers. How many feathers are there in all?

$$3 + 3 + 3 + 3 = \underline{12}$$
$$4 \times 3 = \underline{12}$$

2. There are 3 circus rings. There are 3 elephants in each ring. How many elephants are in the rings?

$$3 + 3 + 3 = \underline{}$$
$$3 \times 3 = \underline{}$$

---

3. There are 5 horses. There are 2 riders on each horse. How many riders are there?

$$2 + 2 + 2 + 2 + 2 = \underline{}$$
$$5 \times 2 = \underline{}$$

4. Tran bought 4 tickets. Each ticket cost $5. How much did he spend?

$$\$5 + \$5 + \$5 + \$5 = \$\underline{}$$
$$4 \times \$5 = \$\underline{}$$

Problem Solving

Write a number sentence. Solve.
Use counters if you need to.

5. The circus was in town for 2 weeks. There were 4 shows each week. How many shows were there in all?

$$\underline{} \times \underline{} = \underline{}$$

6. There are 4 circus tents with 1 clown in each. How many clowns are there?

$$\underline{} \times \underline{} = \underline{}$$

Problem Solving

Choose the Operation

Use cubes.
Write a number sentence to solve.

1. A toy clown costs $4.
Anna buys 2 clowns.
How much money does
she spend?

$$\underline{2} \,\, \underline{\textcircled{\times}} \,\, \underline{4} = \underline{8}$$

$$\$ \,\, \underline{8}$$

2. Owen draws 21 circus
pictures. Julie draws 16
pictures. How many more
pictures does Owen
draw than Julie?

$$\underline{} \,\, \bigcirc \,\, \underline{} = \underline{}$$

_____ more pictures

3. Nancy ate 8 peanuts.
Paul ate 9 peanuts. Lita
ate 7 peanuts. Altogether,
how many peanuts did
they eat?

$$\underline{} \,\, \bigcirc \,\, \underline{} \,\, \bigcirc \,\, \underline{} = \underline{}$$

_____ peanuts

4. Jay has 5 toy circus
tents. He puts 4 toy
tigers in each. How many
tigers are there?

$$\underline{} \,\, \bigcirc \,\, \underline{} = \underline{}$$

_____ tigers

Story Corner

5. Tell a friend a story about
the picture. Make up a
problem. Have your friend
write a number sentence to
solve it.

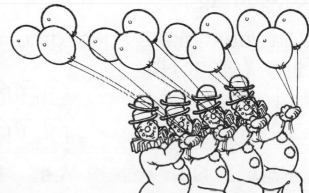

$$\underline{} \,\, \bigcirc \,\, \underline{} = \underline{}$$

Exploring Division: Sharing

Use counters.
Show how many are in each group.

1.

Ring 2 equal groups.
How many are in each

group? _2_

2.

Ring 3 equal groups.
How many are in each

group? ____

3.

Ring 3 equal groups.
How many are in each

group? ____

4.

Ring 2 equal groups.
How many are in each

group? ____

Reasoning

Can you make 2 equal groups?
Ring **Yes** or **No**.

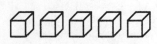      

Yes   No   Yes   No   Yes   No

Exploring Division: Separating

Use counters.
Show how many groups.

1.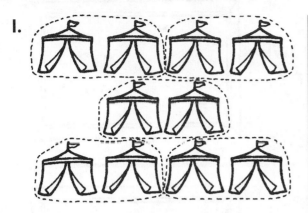

Ring groups of 2.

How many groups? _5_

2.

Ring groups of 4.

How many groups? ____

3.

Ring groups of 3.

How many groups? ____

4.

Ring groups of 5.

How many groups? ____

Reasoning

5. How many clowns can wear

   8 shoes? ____

6. How many shoes are needed

   for 5 clowns? ____

Problem-Solving Strategy

Draw a Picture

Draw a picture to solve.

1. There are 9 fish.
   There are 3 fish in each fishbowl.
   How many fishbowls are there?

   _3_ fishbowls

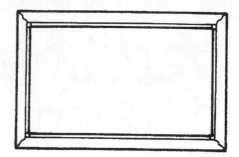

2. There are 12 pillows.
   There are 4 pillows on each sofa.
   How many sofas are there?

   _____ sofas

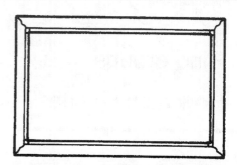

3. There are 15 crayons.
   There are 3 crayons in each box.
   How many boxes are there?

   _____ boxes

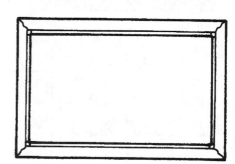

Reasoning

Ring the answer. Then draw a picture to check.

4. You have 20 stickers. Which would use more pages?

   putting 4 stickers on each page

   putting 5 stickers on each page

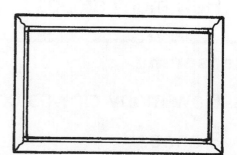

148

Core Skills: Math, Grade 2, Answer Key

Page 1
1. 9
2. 8
3. 9
4. 8
5. 7
6. 8
7. 6
8. 6
9. 9 + 5

Page 2
1. 8; 8; 10; 10; 10; 10
2. 8; 10; 13; 5; 8; 10
3. 6; 12; 9; 4; 9; 9
4. Ring middle train.
5. Ring top train.

Page 3
1. 3 + 6 = 9
2. 8 + 2 = 10
3. 0 + 3 = 3
4. 1 + 6 = 7
5. 6 + 3 = 9
6. 5 + 4 = 9
7. 5 + 3 = 8; 8

Page 4
1. 10; 7; 7; 11; 8; 11
2. 10; 8; 8; 6; 10; 9
3. 4; 5; 3; 12; 10; 5
4. 5; 6; 7; 6; 9; 9
5. 4
6. 7

Page 5
1. ring 5; 7; ring 8; 9; ring 5; 8; ring 6; 7; ring 7; 9; ring 7; 10
2. ring 4; 5; ring 4; 7; ring 4; 6; ring 9; 10; ring 6; 8; ring 8; 10
3. ring 9; 11; ring 7; 8; ring 8; 11; ring 6; 9; ring 5; 8; ring 4; 6
4. ring 9; 12; ring 7; 10; ring 6; 9; ring 8; 10; ring 5; 6; ring 3; 4
5. 9
6. 16

Page 6
1. 3 + 2 = 5; 5
2. 5 + 2 = 7; 7
3. 6 + 3 = 9; 9
4. 4 + 3 = 7; 7
5. Answers may vary. Possible answer: 2 + 2 = 4; 4

Page 7
1. 1 + 4 = 5
2. 5 − 4 = 1
3. 2 + 3 = 5
4. 5 − 3 = 2
5. 5 + 2 = 7
6. 7 − 2 = 5
7. 3 + 3 = 6
8. 6 − 3 = 3
9. 10 + 4 = ?

Page 8
1. 3 − 3 − 0; 5 − 0 = 5; 4 − 4 = 0
2. 6 − 0 = 6; 7 − 7 = 0; 9 − 9 = 0
3. 4 − 0 = 4; 6 − 6 = 0; 8 − 0 = 8
4. 8 − 8 = 0; 7 − 0 = 7; 1 − 0 = 1
5. 0; 3; 0; 9; 0
6. 5 − 5 = 0

Page 9
1. 5 + 3 = 8
2. 8 − 3 = 5
3. 6 − 2 = 4
4. 4 + 2 = 6
5. Ring top number line.

Page 10
1. 4; 7; 4; 2; 8
2. 6; 2; 6; 1; 9; 3
3. 7; 5; 8; 1; 5; 3
4. 4 − 2 = 2; 2
5. 6 − 1 = 5; 5

Page 11
1. 8
2. 5
3. 6
4. 7
5. 7; 8; 7; 6; 6; 9
6. 0
7. 0

Page 12
1–4. Ring the bottom numbers.
1. 2; 1; 1; 3; 2; 1
2. 3; 1; 2; 3; 1; 3
3. 2; 2; 1; 1; 3; 2
4. 3; 1; 2; 2; 2; 3
5. 8

Page 13
1–4. Orders may vary.
1. 7 + 3 = 10; 3 + 7 = 10; 10 − 3 = 7; 10 − 7 = 3
2. 1 + 7 = 8; 7 + 1 = 8; 8 − 1 = 7; 8 − 7 = 1
3. 6 + 1 = 7; 1 + 6 = 7; 7 − 1 = 6; 7 − 6 = 1

4. 4 + 2 = 6; 2 + 4 = 6; 6 − 2 = 4; 6 − 4 = 2
5. 2

Page 14
1. 9 − 2 = 7; 7
2. 4 + 6 = 10; 10
3. 10 − 4 = 6; 6
4. 8 − 4 = 4; 4

Page 15
1. 2; 14; 4; 16; 8; 10
2. 0; 6; 12; 2; 16; 14
3. 5; 10; 8; 9; 6; 10.
   Ring 4 + 4 = 8; 3 + 3 = 6; and 5 + 5 = 10.
4. 4
5. 6

Page 16
1. 8; 4 + 5 = 9; 3 + 4 = 7; 6; 6 + 5 = 11; 10
2. 6 + 7 = 13; 12; 4; 2 + 3 = 5; 16; 9 + 8 = 17
3. 7, yellow; 6, blue; 4, blue; 15, yellow; 13, yellow; 8, blue
4. Ring the second and fourth pictures.

Page 17
1. 14; 14
2. 12; 12
3. 17; 17
4. 13; 15; 16; 17; 12
5. Ring first and last ones.
6. Ring first and second ones.

Page 18
1. 13; 12; 12; 13; 15; 13
2. 11; 14; 14; 15; 11; 13
3. 11; 12; 12; 16; 14; 14
4. 7 − 5 = 2; 2
5. 6 + 7 = 13; 13

Page 19
1. 11; 12; 11; 13; 14
2. 17; 17; 14; 17; 15; 13
3. 16; 15; 16; 19; 18; 14
4–8. Ring numbers 4, 6, and 7.

Page 20
1–4. Addends will vary.
1. 9, 14; 8, 14; 7, 14; 14
2. 9, 13; 8, 13; 7, 13; 13
3. 9, 12; 8, 12; 7, 12; 12
4. 9, 11; 8, 11; 7, 11; 11
5. 3 + 7; 2 + 7

149

Core Skills: Math, Grade 2, Answer Key (cont.)

Page 21
1. 5 + 5 = 10
2. 8 − 6 = 2
3. 11 − 2 = 9
4. 5 + 7 = 12
5. Sample answer: 7 − 4 = 3.

Page 22
1. 13; 14; 12; 13; 17; 12
2. 14; 11; 14; 14; 15; 13
3. 12; 18; 11; 13; 16; 12
4. 17; 11; 12; 11; 12; 11
5. 11 − 8 = 3; 3
6. 5 + 8 = 13; 13

Page 23
1. 12, 6
2. 10, 5
3. 18, 9
4. 4, 2
5. 6, 3
6. 14, 7
7. 8, 4
8. 16, 8
9. 6 + 6 = 12; 12
10. 12 − 6 = 6; 6

Page 24
Check answers.
1. 9
2. 13
3. 6
4. 13

Page 25
1. 9, 7, 8; 6, 9, 8; 7, 9, 8; 8, 6, 2
2. 8, 4, 6; 1, 6, 9; 6, 9, 2; 9, 6, 8
3. 4, 9, 3; 5, 3, 7; 2, 8, 7; 8, 7, 3
4. 6 + 7 = 13; 13
5. 12 − 3 = 9; 9

Page 26
1. 7; 15; 7 + 7 = 14; 15; 8
2. 16; 16; 7; 7; 9 + 9 = 18
3. 8; 9; 17; 9; 16 − 8 = 8
4. 15 − 9 = 6; 6; 8; 14; 14
5. 6 + 6 = 12; 12 − 6 = 6

Page 27
1. 16; 9; 16
2. 13; 5; 13
3. 11; 6; 11
4. 14; 9; 11; 18; 7; 7
5. 8; 8; 13; 15; 5; 12

6. 5 + 5 = 10; 10
7. 5 + 6 = 11; 11

Page 28
1. Cross out, "Josh has 6 sea plants." 12 − 5 = 7; 7
2. Cross out, "Kara has 4 fishing poles." 2 + 8 = 10; 10
3. Cross out, "There are 12 boats." 9 + 8 = 17; 17
4. Cross out, "Yesterday Marta found 4 crabs." 11 − 6 = 5; 5
5. 6 + 4 = 10 or 10 − 6 = 4 or 10 − 4 = 6 or 6 − 4 = 2

Page 29
1. 1; 10
2. 2; 20
3. 4; 40
4. 5; 50
5. 6; 60
6. 8; 80
7. 7 tens
8. 50

Page 30
1. 2 groups of 10 ringed; 2; 3; 23
2. 3 groups of 10 ringed; 3; 2; 32
3. 4 groups of 10 ringed; 4; 8; 48
4. 4 groups of 10 ringed; 4; 1; 41
5. 2 groups of 10 ringed; 2; 9; 29
6. 2 groups of 10 ringed; 2; 6; 26
7. Ring the group in rows.

Page 31
1. 34; 43; 40
2. 32; 14; 4
3. 21; 24; 30
4. 25
5. 74

Page 32
1. 85; 62
2. 87
3. 63
4. 59
5. 86
6. 92; 65; 38
7. 76; 84; 39
8. Fewer than 30.

Page 33
1–4. Check work.
5. Ring the second group.

Page 34
1–2. Consult calendar for next month.
3. 5; 10; 15; 20; counting by fives

Page 35
1. 43; 64; 79
2. 22; 37; 83
3. 13; 86; 65
4. 59; 94; 73
5. 74
6. 20
7. 55

Page 36
1. Check work.
2. ninth
3. fifteenth

Page 37
Table: 2; 3; 12; 13; 22; 23; 32; 33; 42; 43; 52; 53; 62; 63; 72; 73; 82; 83; 92; 93
1. purple rings: 3, 6, 9, 12, 15, 18, 21, 24, 27, 30
2. green rings: 2, 4, 6, 8, 10, 12, 14, 16, 18, 20, 22, 24, 26, 28, 30
3. 51; 61

Page 38
1. 55; 45; 25; 15
2. 17; 21; 25; 29
3. 39; 37; 33; 31
4. 14; 17; 20; 23; 26
5. 54; 64; 74; 84; 94
6–7. Answers will vary.

Page 39
1. red
2. blue
3. blue
4. red
5. blue
6. red
7. red: 32, 6, 48, 22; blue: 3, 7, 25, 13, 41
8. Ring even number.

Core Skills: Math, Grade 2, Answer Key (cont.)

Page 40
1. ring 15; 12
2. 41; ring 49
3. ring 4; 7
4. 30; ring 8
5. 20; ring 11
6. ring 46; 52
7. 75
8. 66

Page 41
1. >; <; <
2. >; >; <
3. <; <; >
4. >; <; >
5–9. Answers will vary.

Page 42
1. 20 coins; 3; 4; 10; 15; 20
2. 6 coins; 4; 5; 6; 16; 20; 24
3. 30 coins

Page 43
1. 2; 3; 4; 5; 6
2. 10; 15; 20; 25; 30
3. 30; 35; 40; 45
4. Press 3 + = = = and so on.

Page 44
1. 5; 10; 15; 16; 16
2. 10; 20; 30; 31; 31
3. 10; 15; 20; 25; 26; 26
4. 10; 20; 30; 40; 45; 46; 46
5. 5¢, 5¢, 5¢
6. 10¢, 10¢, 10¢, 10¢

Page 45
1. 25; 35; 40; 41; 41
2. 25; 30; 35; 36; 37; 37
3. 25; 35; 45; 50; 55; 55
4. 25; 35; 40; 41; 42; 43; 43
5. 36¢
6. 7¢ more

Page 46
1. 31; 25; ring 36
2. ring 35; 27; 25
3. 40; 30; ring 41
4. Tina

Page 47
1. ring Nancy; 50
2. 45
3. 31
4. ring Alan, 50
5. ring Rita; 51
6. 49
7. No correct answer.

Page 48
1. 27
2. 13
3. 17
4. 40
5. 16
6. 55
7. Stories will vary.

Page 49
1. 50; 75; 80; 85; 85
2. 50; 55; 56; 57; 57
3. 25; 50; 60; 65; 65
4. 25; 50; 75; 85; 86; 86
5. 3 pennies

Page 50
1. 72
2. 76
3. 62
4. 70
5. 89
6. 81
7. Ring first belt.

Page 51
1–3. Answers may vary.
1. 55; 50¢, 5¢
2. 80; sample answers: 1 half dollar, 1 quarter, 1 nickel or 1 half dollar, 3 dimes or 3 quarters, 1 nickel
3. 40; sample answers: 1 quarter, 1 dime, 1 nickel or 4 dimes or 1 quarter, 3 nickels
4. 51¢

Page 52
1. 60; 70; 12
2. 40; 45; 7
3. 54; 55; 65; 13
4. 25¢, 1¢

Page 53
1. 95; Yes
2. 80; No
3. 81; No
4. 60; Yes
5. more than 50¢

Page 54
1–3. Check work.
4. 6:00

Page 55
1–6. Check work.
7. 3:00

Page 56
1. 9:30; 1:30; 11:00
2. 12:30; 5:00; 4:30
3. 6:00; 7:30; 11:30
4. 8:30

Page 57
1. 5:15; 7:00; 10:45
2. 11:45; 6:30; 8:15
3. 3:45; 5:30; 9:15
4. 8:45
5. 2:30

Page 58
1. 10:30
2. 12:30
3. 2
4. 30
5. 30
6. 1
7. an hour

Page 59
1. 8:15; 8:20; 8:25; 8:30
2. 10:00; 10:01; 10:02; 10:03
3. 5:45; 5:46; 5:47; 5:48
4. 4:30
5. 5:00

Page 60
1. 1 minute
2. 1 hour
3. 1 minute
4. 1 hour
5. minutes
6. hours

Page 61
1–8. Check work.
9. Friday

Page 62
1. 2 eggs, 3 eggs, 4 eggs
2. 5 eggs, 6 eggs, 7 eggs, 8 eggs
3. 9 eggs, 10 eggs, 11 eggs, 12 eggs
4. Ring second glass.

Page 63
1. 15; Yes; 1; 5
2. 9; No; 0; 9
3. 13; Yes; 1; 3
4. 12; Yes; 1; 2
5. 1 ten 3 ones; 13 ones

Core Skills: Math, Grade 2, Answer Key (cont.)

Page 64
1. 11; Yes; 2; 1
2. 12; Yes; 4; 2
3. 9; No; 6; 9
4. 18; Yes; 3; 8
5. 13; Yes; 5; 3
6. 17; 17

Page 65
1. 33; 50; 23; 30
2. 31; 62; 31; 74
3. 53; 42; 62; 34
4. less than 80
5. greater than 80

Page 66
1. 61; 46; 76; 74
2. 39; 51; 53; 60
3. 44
4. 8, 1

Page 67
1. 76; 76; 68; 73; 71; 47
2. 99; 96; 40; 62; 97; 81
3. 76; 80; 22; 45; 83; 93
4. Theo

Page 68
1. 47; 83; 85; 79; 63; 65
2. 52; 44; 82; 76; 51; 59
3. 62; 62; 55; 71; 84; 93
4. 16 + 39 = 55; 55

Page 69
Table: 26; 17; 8; 13
1. 8
2. 30
3. swimming
4. Answers will vary.

Page 70
1. about 60
2. about 80
3. about 70
4. more than 90

Page 71
1. 54 + 39 = 93; 93
2. 39 + 44 = 83; 83
3. jet
4. No

Page 72
1. 12 + 11 = 23; 23
2. 25 + 35 = 60; 60; Ring "The game has 35 red cards."
3. the first number

Page 73
1. Yes; 2; 9
2. Yes; 3; 5
3. Yes; 1; 3
4. No; 3; 1
5. Yes; 4; 3
6. No; 1; 0
7. less than 40

Page 74
1. 36; 31; 22; 41
2. 29; 17; 17; 39
3. 24; 67; 59; 49
4. 59 − 9 = 50; 50
5. 23 − 8 = 15; 15

Page 75
1. 55, No; 41, No; 23, Yes
2. 29, Yes; 28, Yes; 75, Yes
3. 39, Yes: 23, Yes; 91, No
4. 3, 17

Page 76
1. 26, Yes; 12, No; 69, Yes; 23, No
2. 48, Yes; 17, Yes; 72, No; 57, Yes
3. 37, Yes; 79, Yes; 81, No; 72, No
4. 84 − 25 = 59; 59
5. 57 − 25 = 32; 3, 2

Page 77
1. 26, I; 12, 69, 23, SAW; 48, 26, 37, 79, 12, LIONS; 69, 62, AT; 62, 31, 72, THE; 52, 37, 37, ZOO
2. Answers will vary.

Page 78
1. 9 jars colored
2. 10 jars colored
3. 8 jars colored
4. 5 jars colored
5. 18
6. 4
7. 4
8. 2

Page 79
1. 55, 55 + 12 = 67;
   39, 39 + 48 = 87;
   35, 35 + 57 = 92
2. 6, 6 + 77 = 83;
   15, 15 + 30 = 45;
   33, 33 + 21 = 54
3. 29, 29 + 32 = 61;
   52, 52 + 28 = 80;
   17, 17 + 55 = 72

4. 30 − 19 = 11; 11
5. 27 + 15 = 42; 42

Page 80
1. 75 − 67 = 8; 8
2. 67 − 49 = 18; 18
3. 32 + 56 = 88; 88
4. 88 − 40 = 48; 48
5. Answers will vary.

Page 81
1. 52 − 36 = 16; 16
2. 67 + 14 = 81; 81
3. 37 − 13 = 24; 24
4. about 40

Page 82
Check work.

Page 83
1. 92 − 56 = 36; 36
2. 43 + 36 = 79; 79
3. 56 + 43 = 99; 99
4. 79 − 36 = 43; 43
5. 87 − 58 = 29; 29
6. 79 − 47 = 32; 32

Page 84
1. Check coloring.
2. 3; 5; 4; 2; 2; 1
3. Shapes will vary.

Page 85
1. 10
2. 16
3. cone; cylinder
4. cube; rectangular prism

Page 86
1. Check coloring.
2. 2; 5; 4
3. Check coloring.
4. 2; 3; 5
5. circle

Page 87
1–4. Check work.
5. Answers will vary.

Page 88
1. triangle
2. circle
3. square
4. triangle
5. rectangle
6. triangle
7. rectangle

152

Core Skills: Math, Grade 2, Answer Key (cont.)

Page 89
Check drawings.

Page 90
1. 2; 4; 5; 8
2. 10; 15; 20
3. 20
4. 15

Page 91
1–3. Check work.
4. Ring middle and last shapes.

Page 92
1. 8; 3; 2; 0
2. 4; 6; 2; 3
3. 2; 10; 0; 8
4. 6; 4; 5; 7
5. Answers may vary.

Page 93
1–3. Check coloring.
4. No

Page 94
1. 1; 2; 3
2. 5; 5; 3
3. $\frac{2}{8}$; $\frac{2}{4}$; $\frac{3}{10}$
4. $\frac{4}{5}$; $\frac{3}{8}$; $\frac{2}{3}$
5. $\frac{1}{2}$; $\frac{2}{4}$

Page 95
1. 1 green tree, 2 yellow trees
2. 2 orange trees, 1 red tree
3. 2 blue trees, 3 orange trees
4. 4 purple trees, 1 yellow tree
5. 3 green trees, 1 purple tree
6. 4 red trees, 2 blue trees
7. 1 yellow tree, 3 orange trees; 3

Page 96
Answers will vary.

Page 97
1. Drawings will vary, but cake should be divided into sixths.
2. Pictures will vary, but pie should be divided into fourths; $\frac{1}{4}$

Page 98
1. 4
2. 7
3. 6
4. 3
5. Ring first box.

Page 99
1–3. Check work.
4. shorter than 1 foot
5. longer than 1 foot

Page 100
1–3. Measurements will vary.
1. 7 inches
2. 2 inches
3. 5 inches
4. 1 inch

Page 101
1. Ring piano.
2. Ring boot.
3. Ring ship.
4. Ring turkey.
5. Ring skis.
6. Ring van.
7. Ring tennis racket, puppy, and ring.
8. Answers will vary.

Page 102
1. more than 1 pound
2. about 1 pound
3. more than 1 pound
4. less than 1 pound
5. Ring middle picture.
6. Ring last picture.

Page 103
1. Color 2 cups.
2. Color 4 cups.
3. 2
4. 4
5. Beth
6. 3 cups
7. less than 1 quart
8. more than 1 cup

Page 104
1. ruler
2. cup
3. scale
4. ruler
5. Answers will vary.

Page 105
1–3. Check work.
4. Answers will vary.
5. 10

Page 106
1. 6 + 5 + 4 = 15; 15
2. 7 + 3 + 7 + 3 = 20
3. 3 + 6 + 5 + 8 = 22

Page 107
1. 1; 2; 3
2. 5; 1; 2
3. 2 kilograms
4. 1 kilogram

Page 108
1. 12
2. Angie
3. 60
4. 24
5. Ring first picture.

Page 109
1–4. Answers will vary.
5. 30 degrees Fahrenheit

Page 110
1–3. Guesses will vary.
1. 10
2. 6
3. 6

Page 111
1. 200
2. 400
3. 600
4. 800
5. 900
6. 700
7. 500
8. 300
9. 100
10. 400
11. 400

Page 112
1. 3, 2, 4; 324
2. 5, 6, 1; 561
3. 4, 3, 5; 435
4. 8
5. 40
6. 200
7. 3

Page 113
1–2. Check tables.
3. Ring top two models.

Page 114
1. 5, 4, 3; 543
2. 6, 8, 2; 682
3. 4, 8, 7; 487
4. 3, 8, 5; 385
5. 2, 6, 1, 261
6. 1, 9, 0; 190
7. 183
8. 831

Core Skills: Math, Grade 2, Answer Key (cont.)

Page 115
1. 7, 2, 8, 700, 20, 8; 2, 7, 8; 200, 70, 8
2. 5, 1, 6, 500, 10, 6; 6, 5, 1, 600, 50, 1
3. 4, 3, 7, 400, 30, 7; 3, 4, 7, 300, 40, 7
4. 907
5. 620

Page 116
1. 487
2. 552
3. 807
4. 611
5. Across:
   1. 200
   2. 450
   4. 9
   5. 718
   6. 456
   9. 789
   11. 573
   13. 500
   14. 16
   15. 998
   Down:
   1. 294
   2. 417
   3. 588
   7. 555
   8. 670
   10. 906
   12. 309
   14. 18
6. 340

Page 117
1–2. Answers will vary.
3. shortest bar

Page 118
1. 334, 550, 386
2. 242, 710, 401
3. 693, 376, 248
4. 598, 319, 200
5. 563, 376, 873
6. 364, 543, 300
7. Draw diamond, heart.
8. Draw diamond, diamond.

Page 119
1. Ring 314; 431
2. Ring 453; 543
3. Ring 203; 302
4. 330; ring 303
5. Ring 167, 478, 823, 323, 109

Page 120
1. <, <, <
2. >, <, >
3. >, <, >
4. <, >, >
5. <, >, >
6. 27, 56, 98, 109, 129; 82, 208, 280, 802, 820

Page 121
1. 20, 40, 60, 80, 100
2. 67, 77, 87
3. 109, 209, 309
4. 250
5. 930

Page 122
1–5. Answers will vary.
6. Ring second and third drawings.

Page 123
1–4. Check work.
5. $1.15; ring $1.25
6. Yes

Page 124
1. Ring second question.
2. Ring first question.
3. Accept reasonable responses.
4. Answers will vary.

Page 125
1. 4, 5, 6, 7, 8, 9
2. 40, 50, 60, 70, 80, 90
3. 400, 500, 600, 700, 800, 900
4. 900, 800, 700, 600, 500, 400
5. The top equation matches the top model; and the bottom equation matches the bottom model.

Page 126
1. 481, 399, 770
2. 732, 598, 873
3. The sum is > 500.
4. The sum is < 900.

Page 127
1. 739, 545, 564
2. 391, 479, 461
3. 881, 380, 629
4. 329 + 221 = 550; 550
5. 102 + 89 = 191; 191

Page 128
1. 437, 580, 489
2. 660, 919, 933
3. 916, 908, 894, 622, 798, 809
4. 640
5. 336

Page 129
1. 783, 697, 915, 958, 728
2. 560, 649, 955, 817, 572
3. 879, 183, 985, 749, 766
4. 134 + 290 = 424; 424
5. 236 + 328 = 564; 564

Page 130
1–4. Check graph.
5. 0

Page 131
1. 1, 2, 3, 4, 5, 6
2. 10, 20, 30, 40, 50, 60
3. 100, 200, 300, 400, 500, 600
4. 400
5. 900
6. The top equation matches the bottom model; and the bottom equation matches the top model.

Page 132
1. 117, 224, 559
2. 328, 318, 316
3. 205, 318, 422
4. The difference is > 300.
5. The difference is < 300.

Page 133
1. 439, 448, 665
2. 528, 129, 311
3. 507, 216, 439, 621, 226
4. 352 − 218 = 134; 134
5. 250 − 32 = 218; 218

Page 134
1. 194, 393, 217
2. 320, 371, 390
3. 916, 400, 131, 132, 316
4. 345; she
5. 115

Page 135
1. $1.00, $4.00, $4.00, $3.00
2. $5.00, $5.06; $7.00, $6.54; $5.00, $5.47
3. $2.00, $2.00, $1.00

Core Skills: Math, Grade 2, Answer Key (cont.)

Page 136
1. $1.00 + $1.00 = $2.00; No
2. $4.00 + $3.00 = $7.00; No
3. $4.00 + $1.00 = $5.00; Yes
4. The change is < $1.00.

Page 137
1–4. Check drawings.
5. Ring first hat.

Page 138
1. Ring all shoes. 6, 6, 3, 6
2. Ring all shoes. 8, 8, 4, 8
3. Ring all shoes. 4, 4, 2, 4
4. Ring all shoes. 10, 10, 5, 10
5. 5 x 5 = 25; 25
6. 5 x 3 = 15; 15

Page 139
1. Ring money horizontally.
   2, 6
2. Ring money horizontally.
   5, 15
3. Ring money vertically. 4, 16
4. Ring money horizontally.
   2, 8
5. 4 stacks of 5 umbrellas

Page 140
1. 4 x 2 = 8; 2 x 4 = 8
2. 3 x 5 = 15; 5 x 3 = 15
3. 3 x 4 = 12; 4 x 3 = 12
4. 2 x 3 = 6; 3 x 2 = 6
5. 4 x 4 = 16; 4 x 4 = 16
6. 5 x 2 = 10; 2 x 5 = 10
7. Facts will vary.

Page 141
1. 3
2. 4
3. 20
4. 8
5. 2, 5, 4, 1, 3
6. 0 cubes
7. 0 apples

Page 142
1. 12
2. 16
3. C
4. 28
5. No
6. 8 children

Page 143
1. 4 x 5 = 20
2. 5 x 4 = 20
3. 1 x 4 = 4
4. 4 x 1 = 4
5. 3 x 5 = 15
6. 5 x 3 = 15
7. Answers will vary.

Page 144
1. 12, 12
2. 9, 9
3. 10, 10
4. 20, 20
5. 2 x 4 = 8
6. 4 x 1 = 4

Page 145
1. 2 x 4 = 8; 8
2. 21 − 16 = 5; 5
3. 8 + 9 + 7 = 24; 24
4. 5 x 4 = 20; 20
5. Answers will vary.

Page 146
1–4. Check work.
1. 2
2. 1
3. 4
4. 5
5. No, Yes, No

Page 147
1–4. Check work.
1. 5
2. 2
3. 3
4. 2
5. 4
6. 10

Page 148
1–3. Check work.
1. 3
2. 3
3. 5
4. putting 4 stickers on
   each page